Milton

GOLDENTREE BIBLIOGRAPHIES
In Language and Literature
under the series editorship of
O. B. Hardison, Jr.

Milton

SECOND EDITION

compiled by

James Holly Hanford

and

William A. McQueen

*University of North Carolina
at Chapel Hill*

AHM Publishing Corporation
Arlington Heights, Illinois 60004

PRINTED IN THE UNITED STATES OF AMERICA
729

Contents

CONTENTS

Preface

The following bibliography is intended for graduate and advanced undergraduate students in courses on Milton and related subjects who desire a convenient guide to Miltonic scholarship. The listing is necessarily selective, but every effort has been made to provide ample coverage of the major works and topics, with emphasis on work published in the twentieth century.

In order to keep this bibliography to a practical size, a great number of pertinent references had to be left out. With a bare handful of exceptions in two or three categories, the classes of excluded references are as follows:

School editions.

Short articles on minor points.

Popular and semi-popular books and articles.

Unpublished doctoral dissertations.

In general, the compilers have attempted to steer a middle course between the brief lists of references included in the average textbook and the long professional bibliography in which significant items are often lost in the sheer number of references given. This bibliography should materially assist the student in his efforts to survey a topic, write reports and term papers, prepare for examinations, and do independent reading.

Attention is called to the following features intended to enhance the book's utility:

1. All items are numbered consecutively throughout the book. Thus each title can be readily identified by its own number, both in the cross-reference and in the index.
2. Wide margins on each page provide space for listing the call numbers of frequently used references.
3. Extra space at the bottom of each page can be used for additional references and pertinent notes.
4. More space is provided for personal annotations and comments on the blank pages, headed "Notes," following the index.

5. For some entries the following additional information is given:

   a. The publishers and dates of publication of reprints and paperback editions. Paperback editions are followed by a dagger (+).

   b. Cross-references to other entries in the bibliography.

   c. Brief descriptions of the contents of works cited when clarification seems needed.

Note by the Second Compiler

I have tried to keep in mind the high standards that Professor Hanford set in everything that he did. Some of his entries have been rearranged and some items that he overlooked have been added, but only a very few of his entries have been omitted.

A time gap between the compilation and the publication of the bibliography has necessitated the omission of some excellent recent studies. I particularly regret that I was unable to include entries for the first three volumes of the *Milton Encyclopedia* (Bucknell University Press, 1978) and for Roland Frye's *Milton's Imagery and the Visual Arts* (Princeton University Press, 1978). These works could be written by hand as 16 A (under the name of the general editor, William B. Hunter, Jr.) and 1511 C respectively. Bibliographies, of course, can never be perfectly current, and this one, unfortunately, is no exception. At some point one simply has to stop and leave the proliferating materials for a later effort.

Abbreviations

Abbreviations for journals cited generally follow the standard forms given at the beginning of recent PMLA bibliographies. The abbreviations and their meanings are as follows:

AJP   American Journal of Philology
AnM   Annuale Mediaevale
BJRL   Bulletin of the John Rylands Library
BNYPL   Bulletin of the New York Public Library
BSTCF   Ball State Teacher's College Forum
BSUF   Ball State University Forum
CE   College English
EA   Études Anglaises
E&S   Essays and Studies by Members of the English Association
EC   Études Celtiques
EHR   English Historical Review
EIC   Essays in Criticism
ELH   Journal of English Literary History
ELN   English Language Notes
ELR   English Literary Renaissance
EM   English Miscellany
ES   English Studies
EUQ   Emory University Quarterly
FMod   Filología Moderna
HLQ   Huntington Library Quarterly
HTR   Harvard Theological Review
HudR   Hudson Review
JEGP   Journal of English and Germanic Philology
JHI   Journal of the History of Ideas
JHM   Journal of the History of Medicine
JRUL   Journal of the Rutgers University Library
JWCI   Journal of the Warburg and Courtauld Institute
KR   Kenyon Review
Libr.   The Library
MCR   Melbourne Critical Review
MLN   Modern Language Notes
MLQ   Modern Language Quarterly
MLR   Modern Language Review
Milton N Milton Newsletter

ABBREVIATIONS

Milton Q Milton Quarterly
MP   Modern Philology
MQ   Midwest Quarterly
N&Q   Notes and Queries
Neophil   Neophilologus
PAPS   Proceedings of the American Philosophical Society
PBSA   Papers of the Bibliographical Society of America
PMASAL   Papers of the Michigan Academy of Sciences, Arts, and Letters
PMLA   Publications of the Modern Language Association of America
PQ   Philological Quarterly
PR   Partisan Review
PULC   Princeton University Library Chronicle
RECTR   Restoration and 18th Century Theatre Research
RES   Review of English Studies
RN (RQ)   Renaissance News (Now Renaissance Quarterly)
SA   Studi Americani
SAQ   South Atlantic Quarterly
SCN   Seventeenth-Century News
SEL   Studies in English Literature, 1500–1900
SN   Studia Neophilologica
SoQ   The Southern Quarterly
SP   Studies in Philology
SPCK   Society for Promoting Christian Knowledge
SR   Sewanee Review
TLS   [London] Times Literary Supplement
TRSC   Transactions of the Royal Society of Canada
TSE   Tulane Studies in English
TSLL   Texas Studies in Literature and Language
UTQ   University of Toronto Quarterly
UWSLL   University of Wisconsin Studies in Language and Literature
YR   Yale Review

Note: The publisher and compiler invite suggestions for additions to future editions of the bibliography.

Bibliographical and Reference Works

For recent scholarship on Milton, the annual bibliographies in PMLA (25) will be most useful. Huckabay (14) provides a cumulative bibliography for the period 1929–1968, and Stevens (35) covers the period 1800–1928. For Milton bibliography before 1800 the best single source is Todd's edition (293), which devotes twenty-five pages to a list of editions, translations, and criticism. The most useful topical indexes to Milton's works are Patterson and Fogle's index to the Columbia Milton (30), Thompson's topical bibliography (37), and the "Index and Finding List" in Parker's biography (27). For concordances to the poetry see Ingram and Swaim (17) and Cooper (7). Until the proposed concordance to the prose appears, one will have to make do with the indexes in the Yale edition of the prose and in the Columbia edition of the complete works.

1 BATESON, F. W., ed. *The Cambridge Bibliography of English Literature.* 4 vols. Cambridge: Cambridge Univ. Press, 1940. Supplement 1957, Vol. V. ed. George Watson. [Although this edition is generally superseded by the new edition (see **39**), it contains sections on the Social and Political Background which were not retained in the new edition.]

1A BOSWELL, Jackson C. *Milton's Library.* New York and London: Garland Publishing, Inc., 1975.

2 BRADSHAW, John. *A Concordance to the Poetical Works of John Milton.* London: Sonnenschein, 1894; New York: Macmillan, 1894. [Archon, 1965.]

3 British Museum. Department of Printed Books. *Catalogue of Printed Books. Milton.* London: W. Clowes, 1892.

4 BUSH, Douglas. *English Literature in the Earlier Seventeenth Century 1600–1660.* 2d ed. Oxford: Clarendon Press, 1962. [A literary history of the period with bibliographies on pp. 461–668.]

5 BUSH, Douglas. "Milton." *English Poetry: Select Bibliographical Guides.* Ed. A. E. Dyson. London: Oxford Univ. Press, 1971, pp. 76–95.

6 COLERIDGE, K. A. "Some Amendments to W. R. Parker's Census of Seventeenth-Century Editions of Milton." *N&Q,* 19 (1972), 175–76.

7 COOPER, Lane. *A Concordance of the Latin, Greek, and, Italian Poems of John Milton.* Halle (Saale): M. Niemeyer, 1923; New York: Barnes & Noble, 1963.

8 DAVIES, Godfrey, ed. *Bibliography of British History, Stuart Period, 1603–1714.* Oxford: Clarendon Press, 1928. 2d ed. by Mary Frear Keeler. Oxford: Clarendon Press, 1970.

9 English Association. *The Year's Work in English Studies.* 1920–. [Annual bibliography, published in London.]

10 FLETCHER, Harris Francis. *Contributions to a Milton Bibliography, 1800–1930, Being a List of Addenda to Stevens's Reference Guide to Milton.* Urbana: Univ. of Illinois Press, 1931. [Johnson Reprint Corp., 1968.]

11 GILBERT, Allan H. *A Geographical Dictionary of Milton.* New Haven: Yale Univ. Press, 1919.

BIBLIOGRAPHICAL AND REFERENCE WORKS

12 HOWARD-HILL, T. H. *Bibliography of British Literary Bibliographies.* Oxford: Clarendon Press, 1969. [The list of bibliographies for "Forms and Genres" and "Subjects" may prove useful.]

13 HOWARD-HILL, T. H. *Shakespearian Bibliography and Textual Criticism.* Oxford: Clarendon Press, 1971. [Contains a supplement to *Bibliography of British Literary Bibliographies,* pp. 179–322.]

14 HUCKABAY, Calvin. *John Milton: An Annotated Bibliography 1929–1968.* Rev. ed. Pittsburg: Duquesne Univ. Press; Louvain: E. Nauwelaerts, 1969.

15 HUDSON, Gladys W. *Paradise Lost: A Concordance.* Detroit: Gale Research Co., 1970. [See J. Max Patrick's review in *SCN,* 29 (1971); 64, 66, for comments on its use.]

16 HUGHES, Merritt, gen. ed. *A Variorum Commentary on the Poems of John Milton.* New York: Columbia Univ. Press, 1970-.
   Vol. I: "The Latin and Greek Poems," ed. Douglas Bush; "The Italian Poems," ed. J. E. Shaw and A. Bartlett Giamatti, 1970.
   Vol. II (in 3 parts): "The Minor English Poems," ed. A. S. P. Woodhouse and Douglas Bush. Also includes "Studies of Verse Form in the Minor English Poems," ed. Edward R. Weismiller, pp. 1107–1187, 1972.
   Vol. III: *Paradise Lost,* ed. Merritt Y. Hughes and John M. Steadman, forthcoming.
   Vol. IV: *Paradise Regained,* ed. Walter MacKellar. Also includes "Studies of Style and Verse Form in *Paradise Regained,"* ed. Edward R. Weismiller, pp. 253–363, 1975.
   Vol. V: *Samson Agonistes,* ed. William R. Parker and John M. Steadman, forthcoming.
   Vol. VI: "The Prosody of the English Poems," ed. Edward R. Weismiller, forthcoming.

17 INGRAM, William, and SWAIM, Kathleen. *A Concordance to Milton's English Poetry.* New York: Oxford Univ. Press, 1972. [The standard concordance for Milton's English poetry.]

18 LECOMTE, Edward S. *A Milton Dictionary.* New York: Philosophical Library, 1961.†

19 *Library of Congress Catalog. Books: Subjects.* 1950–1954–to date. Ann Arbor and Washington, D. C., 1955–.

20 LOCKWOOD, Laura E. *Lexicon to the English Poetical Works of John Milton.* New York, London: Macmillan, 1907.

20A *Milton and the Romantics.* Ed. Luther L. Scales, Jr. Statesboro, Georgia: Georgia Southern College. [An annual journal of notes and essays on relationship of the English Romantic poets and Milton.]

21 *Milton Quarterly.* Ed. Roy C. Flanagan. Athens, Ohio: Ohio University, 1967–. [A quarterly publication containing short articles and notes, book reviews, abstracts of recent articles and papers, completed dissertations, work in progress, and news of general interest to Milton scholars.]

22 Milton Society of America. *Annual Dinner and Meeting.* 1955–. [An annual booklet containing bibliographies of scholars who are honored at the yearly meeting, a list of the membership for the year, and an account of work in progress by the members.]

2

23 *Milton Studies.* Ed. James D. Simmonds. Pittsburg: Univ. of Pittsburg Press, 1969–. [An annual publication devoted exclusively to Milton scholarship and criticism.]

24 Modern Humanities Research Association. *Annual Bibliography of English Language and Literature.* 1920–. [Cites book reviews.]

25 Modern Language Association of America. *PMLA: Publications of the Modern Language Association of America.* [Annual bibliographies for the preceding year.]

26 *National Union Catalog Pre-1956 Imprints.* London: Mansell; Chicago: American Library Association, 1975. [Useful for finding the location of particular editions at institutions in the U.S. and Canada. Entries for Milton are found in Vol. 385, pp. 243–392. Supplemented by *National Union Catalog,* 1953–1957–to date. Washington, D.C., 1958–.]

27 PARKER, William Riley. "Index and Finding List." *Milton: A Biography.* Oxford: Clarendon Press, 1968, Vol. II, 1215–1489. [By consulting the Index and Finding List in conjunction with the Notes, one can determine the location of early editions of Milton's works. See the page numbers in boldface type under the desired edition in the Index. See 6.]

28 PATRIDES, C. A. "An Annotated Reading List." *Milton's Epic Poetry.* Baltimore: Penguin, 1967, pp. 381–428.

29 PATRIDES, C. A. "Bibliography." *John Milton: Selected Prose.* Baltimore: Penguin, 1974, pp. 399–426.

30 PATTERSON, Frank A., and FOGLE, French R. *An Index to the Columbia Edition of the Works of John Milton.* 2 vols. New York: Columbia Univ. Press; London: Milford, 1940.

31 DOUGHTIE, Edward, ed. "Recent Studies in the English Renaissance." *SEL.* Houston: Rice University, 1961–. [Contains an annual survey of "Recent Studies in the Renaissance," including comment on selected Milton scholarship.]

32 SACHSE, William L. *Restoration England 1660–1689.* Cambridge: Cambridge Univ. Press, 1971. [Contains an annotated general bibliography for the period.]

33 *Seventeenth-Century News.* Ed. J. Max Patrick and Harrison T. Messerole. University Park, Pa.: Pennsylvania State University, 1942–. [Frequently contains reviews, abstracts, and items of interest to Miltonists.]

34 SOTHEBY, Samuel Leigh. *Ramblings in the Elucidation of the Autograph of Milton.* London: T. Richards, 1861.

35 STEVENS, David Harrison. *A Reference Guide to Milton from 1800 to the Present Day.* Chicago: Univ. of Chicago Press, 1930.

36 SUTHERLAND, James. *English Literature of the Late Seventeenth Century.* New York and Oxford: Oxford Univ. Press, 1969. [A literary history of the period 1660–1700 with bibliographies on pp. 442–578.]

37 THOMPSON, E. N. S. *John Milton: A Topical Bibliography.* New Haven: Yale Univ. Press, 1916.

38 WATSON, George, ed. *The Cambridge Bibliography of English Literature.* Vol. V. Cambridge: Cambridge Univ. Press, 1957. [A supplement of the 1940 edition.]

39 WATSON, George, ed. *The New Cambridge Bibliography of English Literature.* Cambridge: Cambridge Univ. Press, 1969–1974. [Vol. I: 1600–1660; Vol. II: 1660–1800.]

40 WING, Donald. *Short-Title Catalogue of Books Printed in England, Scotland,*

BIBLIOGRAPHICAL AND REFERENCE WORKS

Ireland, Wales, and British America and of English Books Printed in Other Countries 1641–1700. New York: Printed for the Index Society by Columbia Univ. Press, 1945–1951. 3 vols. [Vol. I of a revised edition (A1-E2926) was published by MLA in 1972. (See the review in *TLS,* 26 Jan. 73, p. 100.) The *Short Title Catalogue* is intended for the use of advanced students and scholars who are working with seventeenth-century editions.]

Useful Background Studies

41 ADOLPH, Robert M. *The Rise of Modern Prose Style.* Cambridge: The M.I.T. Press, 1968.

42 ALLEN, Beverly Sprague. *Tides in English Taste (1619–1800): A Background for the Study of Literature.* 2 vols. Cambridge: Harvard Univ. Press, 1937; New York: Pageant Books, 1958. [Contains many pictures.]

43 ALLEN, Don Cameron. *Doubt's Boundless Sea: Skepticism and Faith in the Renaissance.* Baltimore: Johns Hopkins Press, 1964.

43A Allen, Don Cameron. *The Legend of Noah: Renaissance Rationalism in Art, Science, and Letters.* Urbana: Univ. of Illinois Press, 1949. [paperback, 1963]†

44 ALLEN, Don Cameron. *Mysteriously Meant: The Rediscovery of Pagan Symbolism and Allegorical Interpretation in The Renaissance.* Baltimore and London: Johns Hopkins Press, 1970. [Milton is discussed on pp. 289–301.]

44A ALLEN, John William. *English Political Thought, 1603–1644.* Hamden, Conn.: Archon, 1967. [Originally published under a slightly different title, London: Methuen, 1938.]

45 ASHLEY, Maurice. *England in the Seventeenth Century.* Baltimore: Penguin, 1952, 1958, 1961.†

46 ASHLEY, Maurice. *The Golden Century: Europe 1598–1715.* New York and Washington: Praeger, 1969. [Illustrated.]

47 ATKINS, J. W. H. *English Literary Criticism: The Renaissance.* London: Methuen, 1947, 1951.

48 ATKINS, J. W. H. *English Literary Criticism: 17th and 18th Centuries.* London: Methuen, 1951.

49 AYLMER, G. E., ed. *The Interregnum: The Quest for Settlement 1646–1660.* London: Macmillan; Hamden, Conn.: Archon Books, 1972. [A collection of essays on various facets of the Interregnum. Useful bibliographies.]

50 BAKER, Herschel. *The Image of Man: A Study of the Idea of Human Dignity in Classical Antiquity, The Middle Ages, and the Renaissance.* New York: Harper, 1961. [Torchbook]†

51 BAKER, Herschel. *The Wars of Truth: Studies in the Decay of Humanism in the Earlier Seventeenth Century.* London: Staples Press; Cambridge: Harvard Univ. Press, 1952.

52 BALDWIN, T. W. *William Shakespere's Small Latine and Lesse Greeke.* 2 vols. Urbana: Univ. of Illinois Press, 1944. [An extensive examination of the English grammar school curriculum in the sixteenth century, including St. Pauls.]

53 BAROWAY, Israel. "The Bible as Poetry in the English Renaissance." *JEGP,* 32 (1933), 447–480. [Baroway also has three articles on Renaissance theories of Hebrew prosody in *ELH,* 2 (1935), 66–91; 8 (1941), 119–142; 17 (1950), 115–135.]

54 BENNETT, H. S. *English Books and Readers 1603 to 1640: Being a Study of the History of the Book Trade in the Reigns of James I and Charles I.* Cambridge: Cambridge Univ. Press, 1970.

55 BOLGAR, R. R. *The Classical Heritage and Its Beneficiaries: From the Carolingian Age to the End of the Renaissance.* London and New York: Cambridge Univ. Press, 1954. [Torchbook]†

56 BRADNER, Leicester. *Musae Anglicanae: A History of Anglo-Latin Poetry 1500–1925.* New York: Modern Language Association; London: Oxford Univ. Press, 1940. See **57.**

57 BRADNER, Leicester. "*Musae Anglicanae: A Supplemental List.*" *The Library.* 22 (1967), 93–103. *[In addition to listing over 100 new titles, this article contains corrections of errors in the original list and additional information about items found there.]*

58 BRIDENBAUGH, Carl. *Vexed and Troubled Englishmen, 1590–1642.* London: Oxford Univ. Press, 1968.

59 BROWN, Calvin S. *Music and Literature: A Comparison of the Arts.* Athens: Univ. of Ga. Press, 1948.

60 BURNS, Norman T. *Christian Mortalism from Tyndale to Milton.* Cambridge: Harvard Univ. Press, 1972. [See the review by James McAdams in *SCN,* 32 (1974), 4–5.]

61 BUSH, Douglas. *Prefaces to Renaissance Literature.* Cambridge: Harvard Univ. Press. 1965.

62 CAMPBELL, Lily B. "The Christian Muse." *Huntington Library Bulletin,* no. 8 (Oct. 1935), 29–70.

63 CAMPBELL, Lily B. *Divine Poetry and Drama in Sixteenth-Century England.* Cambridge: Cambridge Univ. Press; Berkeley and Los Angeles: Univ. of California Press, 1959.

64 CASSIRER, Ernst. *The Individual and the Cosmos in Renaissance Philosophy.* Trans. Mario Domandi. New York: Harper and Row, 1963. [Pennsylvania]†

65 CHARLTON, Kenneth. *Education in Renaissance England.* London: Routledge & Kegan Paul; Toronto: Univ. of Toronto Press, 1965.

65A CLARENDON, Edward, Earl of. *History of the Rebellion and Civil Wars in England.* Ed. W. Dunn Macray. 6 vols. Oxford: Clarendon Press, 1888.

65B CLARK, Alice. *The Working Life of Women in the Seventeenth Century.* London: Routledge; New York: E. P. Dutton, 1919. [Reprinted New York: A. M. Kelley, 1968.]

66 COLIE, Rosalie. *Paradoxia Epidemica: The Renaissance Tradition of Paradox.* Princeton: Princeton Univ. Press, 1966.

67 COLIE, Rosalie. *The Resources of Kind: Genre-Theory in the Renaissance.* Ed. Barbara K. Lewalski. Berkeley, Los Angeles, London: Univ. of California Press, 1973. [Milton is specifically discussed on pp. 119–122.]

68 COLLINGWOOD, R. G. *The Idea of Nature.* Oxford: Clarendon Press, 1945. [Oxford Paperback]†

69 COOLIDGE, John S. *The Pauline Renaissance in England: Puritanism and the Bible.* Oxford: Clarendon Press, 1970. [Provides an excellent background for understanding Milton's affinities with Paul, although Milton is specifically mentioned only once.]

70 COSTELLO, William T., S. J. *The Scholastic Curriculum at Early Seventeenth-Century Cambridge.* Cambridge: Harvard Univ. Press, 1958.

USEFUL BACKGROUND STUDIES

71 CURTIS, Mark H. *Oxford and Cambridge in Transition 1558–1642: An Essay on Changing Relations between the English Universities and English Society.* Oxford: Clarendon Press, 1959.

72 CURTIUS, Ernst Robert. *European Literature and the Latin Middle Ages.* Trans. Willard R. Trask. New York: Pantheon, 1953. [Torchbook]†

73 DAVIES, Godfrey. *The Early Stuarts, 1603–1660.* 2nd ed. Oxford: Clarendon Press, 1959.

74 DAVIES, Horton. *Worship and Theology in England.* Princeton: Princeton Univ. Press. Vol. I: *From Cranmer to Hooker, 1534–1603* (1970). Vol. II: *From Andrewes to Baxter, 1603–1690* (to be published). Vol. III: *From Watts and Wesley to Maurice, 1690–1850* (1962)

75 DICKENS, A. G. *The English Reformation.* New York: Schocken, 1964.

75A DORANGEON, Simone. *L'Églogue Anglaise de Spenser à Milton.* Paris: Didier, 1974.

76 DURLING, Robert M. *The Figure of the Poet in Renaissance Epic.* Cambridge: Harvard Univ. Press, 1965.

77 FALKUS, Christopher. *The Life and Times of Charles II.* Garden City, New York: Doubleday, 1972. [Profusely illustrated.]

78 FINK, Zera S. *The Classical Republicans: An Essay in the Recovery of a Pattern of Thought.* Evanston, Ill.: Northwestern Univ. Press, 1945, 1962.

79 FINK, Zera S. "Venice and English Political Thought in the Seventeenth Century." *MP,* 38 (1940), 155–172.

80 FINNEY, Gretchen Ludke. *Musical Backgrounds for English Literature: 1580–1650.* New Brunswick, N.J.: Rutgers Univ. Press, 1962.

80A FIRTH, Charles Harding. *The Last Years of the Protectorate, 1656–1658.* 2 vols. New York: Russell & Russell, 1964. [First published 1909.]

81 FISCH, Harold. *Jerusalem and Albion: The Hebraic Factor in Seventeenth-Century Literature.* London: Routledge & Kegan Paul, 1964.

81A FISH, Stanley E. *Self-Consuming Artifacts:* The Experience *of Seventeenth Century Literature.* Berkeley, Los Angeles, London: Univ. of California Press, 1972, [California Paperback, 1974]†

82 FRANK, Joseph. *Hobbled Pegasus: A Descriptive Bibliography of Minor English Poetry, 1641–1660.* Albuquerque: Univ. of New Mexico Press, 1968.

83 FRANK, Joseph. *The Levellers. A History of the Writings of Three Seventeenth-Century Social Democrats: John Lilburne, Richard Overton, and William Walwyn.* Cambridge: Harvard Univ. Press, 1955.

84 FRASER, Antonia. *Cromwell: Our Chief of Men.* London: Weidenfeld & Nicolson, 1973. Reprinted as *Cromwell: The Lord Protector.* New York: Knopf, 1973; Dell paperback, 1975.†

85 GARDINER, Samuel Rawson. *History of the Commonwealth and Protectorate, 1649–1660.* 3 vols. London: Longmans, Green, 1894–1901.

86 GARDINER, Samuel Rawson. *History of England from the Accession of James I. to the Outbreak of the Civil War: 1603–1642.* 10 vols. London: Longmans, Green, 1884–1891. [The authoritative work on which later accounts are largely based.]

87 GARDINER, Samuel Rawson. *History of the Great Civil War, 1642–1649.* 3 vols. London: Longmans, Green, 1886–1891.

88 GIAMATTI, A Bartlett. *The Earthly Paradise and the Renaissance Epic.* Princeton: Princeton Univ. Press, 1966.

89 GOOCH, George Peabody. *English Democratic Ideas in the Seventeenth Century.* Cambridge: Cambridge Univ. Press, 1908. [2d ed. with supplementary notes and appendices by H. J. Laski, 1927.]

90 GOOCH, George Peabody. *Political Thought in England: Bacon to Halifax.* London: Oxford Univ. Press, 1915. [Frequently reprinted.]

91 GORDON, Ian. *The Movement of English Prose.* Bloomington and London: Indiana Univ. Press, 1966.

92 GRABO, Norman S. "The Art of Puritan Devotion." *SCN,* 26 (1968), 7–9.

92A GRANT, W. Leonard. *Neo-Latin Literature and the Pastoral.* Chapel Hill: Univ. of North Carolina Press, 1965.

93 GROS LOUIS, Kenneth R. R. "The Triumph and Death of Orpheus in the English Renaissance." *SEL,* 9 (1969), 63–80. [A survey of the changing versions of Orpheus in the 16th and 17th centuries, ending with Milton.]

94 HALEWOOD, William. *The Poetry of Grace: Reformation Themes and Structures in Seventeenth-Century English Verse.* New Haven: Yale Univ. Press, 1970.

95 HALLER, William. *Foxe's Book of Martyrs and the Elect Nation.* London: Jonathan Cape, 1963.

96 HALLER, William. *Liberty and Reformation in the Puritan Revolution.* New York: Columbia Univ. Press, 1955. [Columbia]†

97 HALLER, William. *The Rise of Puritanism; or, The Way to the New Jerusalem as Set Forth in Pulpit and Press from Thomas Cartwright to John Lilburne and John Milton, 1570–1643.* New York: Columbia Univ. Press, 1938. [Torchbook]†

98 HALLER, William, ed. *Tracts on Liberty in the Puritan Revolution.* 3 vols. New York: Columbia Univ. Press, 1935.

99 HALLER, William, and DAVIES, Godfrey, eds. *The Leveller Tracts, 1647–1653.* New York: Columbia Univ. Press; London: Milford, 1944.

100 HALLER, William, and HALLER, Malleville, "The Puritan Art of Love." *HLQ,* 5 (1942), 235–272. [Especially relevant to Milton's divorce tracts.]

101 HAMILTON, K. G. *The Two Harmonies: Poetry and Prose in the Seventeenth Century.* Oxford: Clarendon Press, 1963.

102 HARBISON, E. Harris. *The Christian Scholar in the Age of the Reformation.* New York: Scribners, 1956.† [Studies of Erasmus, Luther, Calvin, Pico, John Colet, and others.]

103 HARDISON, O. B., Jr. *The Enduring Monument.* Chapel Hill: Univ. of North Carolina Press, 1962.

104 HARDISON, O. B., Jr. *English Literary Criticism: The Renaissance.* New York: Appleton-Century-Crofts, 1963.

105 HAYDN, Hiram. *The Counter-Renaissance.* New York: Harcourt, Brace and World, 1950. [Harbinger]†

106 HENINGER, S. K., Jr. *A Handbook of Renaissance Meteorology, with Particular Reference to Elizabethan and Jacobean Literature.* Durham, N. C.: Duke Univ. Press, 1960.

107 HENINGER, S. K., Jr. *Touches of Sweet Harmony: Pythagorean Cosmology and Renaissance Poetics.* San Marino, Calif.: Huntington Library, 1974.

108 HIGHET, Gilbert. *The Classical Tradition: Greek and Roman Influences on Western Literature.* New York: Oxford Univ. Press, 1949. [Galaxy, 1957]†

108A HILL, Christopher. *The Century of Revolution, 1603–1714.* Edinburgh: T. Nelson, 1961. [Norton, 1966]†

109 HILL, Christopher. *God's Englishman: Oliver Cromwell and the English Revolution.* New York: Dial Press, 1970. [Penguin]†

110 HILL, Christopher. *Intellectual Origins of the English Revolution.* Oxford: Clarendon Press, 1965.

111 HILL, Christopher. *Puritanism and Revolution: Studies in the Interpretation of the English Revolution of the 17th Century.* New York: Schocken, 1958. [Schocken.]†

111A HOLLAND, Norman N. "Transactive Criticism: Recreation through Identy." *Criticism,* 18 (1976), 334-352. [A representative example of Holland's interest in the relationships between the reader and the text. Other works of Holland are cited.]

112 HOLLANDER, John. *The Untuning of the Sky: Ideas of Music in English Poetry 1500–1700.* Princeton: Princeton Univ. Press, 1961. [Norton]†

113 HOOPES, Robert. *Right Reason in the English Renaissance.* Cambridge: Harvard Univ. Press, 1962.

114 HOWELL, Wilbur Samuel. *Logic and Rhetoric in England, 1500–1700.* Princeton: Princeton Univ. Press, 1956; New York: Russell & Russell, 1961.

115 JONES, I. Deane. *The English Revolution 1603–1714.* London: Heinemann, 1931. [Reprinted frequently.]

116 JONES, Richard Foster. *Ancients and Moderns: A Study of the Rise of the Scientific Movement in Seventeenth-Century England.* St. Louis: Washington Univ. Press, 1961. [California]†

117 JORDAN, W. K. *The Development of Religious Toleration in England.* 4 vols. Cambridge: Harvard Univ. Press, 1932–1940; Gloucester, Mass.: Peter Smith, 1965.

118 JOSEPH, Sister Miriam, C. S. C. *Rhetoric in Shakespeare's Time.* New York and Burlingame: Harcourt, Brace and World, 1962. [Harbinger]†

119 KEARNEY, Hugh. *Scholars and Gentlemen: Universities and Society in Pre-Industrial Britain, 1500–1700.* Ithaca: Cornell Univ. Press, 1970.

120 KERMODE, Frank. *The Sense of an Ending: Studies in the Theory of Fiction.* London, Oxford, New York: Oxford Univ. Press, 1966, 1967.†

120A KINSMAN, Robert S., ed. *The Darker Vision of the Renaissance: Beyond the Fields of Reason.* Berkeley, Los Angeles, London: Univ. of California Press, 1974.

121 KLIGER, Samuel. *The Goths in England: A Study in Seventeenth and Eighteenth Century Thought.* Cambridge: Harvard Univ. Press, 1952.

122 KOLVE, V. A. *The Play Called Corpus Christi.* Stanford: Stanford Univ. Press, 1966.

123 KRAILSHEIMER, A. J., et al. *The Continental Renaissance 1500–1600.* Baltimore: Penguin, 1971.†

123A LAMBERT, Ellen Zetzel. *Placing Sorrow: A Study of the Pastoral Elegy Convention from Theocritus to Milton.* Chapel Hill: Univ. of North Carolina Press, 1976.

9

124 LAMONT, William M. *Marginal Prynne 1600–1669.* London: Routledge & Kegan Paul; Toronto: Univ. of Toronto Press, 1963.

125 LEVIN, Harry. *The Myth of the Golden Age in the Renaissance.* Bloomington and London: Indiana Univ. Press, 1969.

126 LEWIS, C. S. *The Discarded Image: An Introduction to Medieval and Renaissance Literature.* Cambridge: Cambridge Univ. Press, 1964.

126A LEWIS, C. S. *Studies in Words.* Cambridge: Cambridge Univ. Press, 1960, 1967, 1974.† [A Study of the historical meaning of words such as *nature, free, simple, conscience.*]

127 MACADOO, Henry R. *The Spirit of Anglicanism: A Survey of Anglican Theological Method in the Seventeenth Century.* New York: Scribner's, 1965.

128 MACLURE, Millar. *The Paul's Cross Sermons, 1534–1642.* Toronto: Univ. of Toronto Press, 1958.

129 MARTZ, Louis L. *The Poetry of Meditation: A Study in English Religious Literature of the Seventeenth Century.* New Haven: Yale Univ. Press; London: Oxford Univ. Press, 1954. [Yale]†

130 MAZZEO, Joseph Anthony. *Renaissance and Revolution: Backgrounds to Seventeenth-Century English Literature.* New York: Pantheon, 1965. [Paperback, 1967]†

131 MEAD, Lucia Ames. *Milton's England.* London and Boston: L. C. Page, 1903.

132 MELLERS, Wilfrid. *Harmonious Meeting: A Study of the Relationship between English Music, Poetry, and Theatre, c. 1600–1900.* London: Dennis Dobson, 1965. [Contains a chapter on "Henry Lawes and the Caroline Ayre" and a very general four-page commentary on *Comus.*]

133 MILLER, Perry. *The New England Mind: The Seventeenth Century.* New York: Macmillan, 1939; Cambridge: Harvard Univ. Press, 1954. [Beacon]†

134 MILLER, Perry, and JOHNSON, Thomas H. "General Introduction." *The Puritans: A Sourcebook of Their Writings.* Vol. I, pp. 1–79. New York: Harper and Row, 1963. [Torchbook]†

134A MINER, Earl, ed. *Illustrious Evidence: Approaches to English Literature of the Early Seventeenth Century.* Berkeley: Univ. of California Press, 1975. [A Collection of six essays by Frank L. Huntley, James Thorpe, Barbara Lewalski, Robert M. Adams, Louis L. Martz, and Stanley Fish.]

135 MITCHELL, W. F. *English Pulpit Oratory from Andrewes to Tillotson.* London: SPCK, 1932.

136 MORE, Paul Elmer, and CROSS, Frank Leslie. *Anglicanism: The Thought and Practice of the Church of England, Illustrated from the Religious Literature of the Seventeenth Century.* Milwaukee: Morehouse, 1935. [An anthology of Anglican writing from 1594 to 1691.]

137 MULDER, John R. *The Temple of the Mind: Education and Literary Taste in Seventeenth-Century England.* New York: Pegasus, 1969.†

138 MULLINGER, J. Bass. *History of the University of Cambridge.* London: Longmans, Green, 1888.

139 O'BRIEN, Gordon W. *Renaissance Poetics and the Problem of Power.* Chicago: Institute of Elizabethan Studies, 1956.

140 OGG, David. *Europe in the Seventeenth Century.* 8th ed. New York: Collier Books, 1962.†

USEFUL BACKGROUND STUDIES

141 ONG, Walter J., S. J. *Ramus: Method, and the Decay of Dialogue.* Cambridge: Harvard Univ. Press, 1958.

142. PARKES, Joan. *Travel in England in the Seventeenth Century.* London: Oxford Univ. Press, 1925, 1968.

143 PATRICK, J. Max, et al., eds. *Style, Rhetoric, and Rhythm: Essays by Morris W. Croll.* Princeton: Princeton Univ. Press, 1966. [Princeton, 1969]†

144 PATRIDES, C. A. *The Grand Design of God: The Literary Form of the Christian View of History.* London: Routledge & Kegan Paul, 1972. [A "much amplified version" of *The Phoenix and the Ladder.*]

145 PATRIDES, C. A. *The Phoenix and the Ladder: The Rise and Decline of the Christian View of History.* Berkeley and Los Angeles: Univ. of Calif. Press, 1964.

146 PATTERSON, Annabel. *Hermogenes and the Renaissance: Seven Ideas of Style.* Princeton: Princeton Univ. Press, 1970. [Ch. 1 "Decorum of Style"; Ch. 7 " 'The Grand Master-Piece to Observe' : Renaissance Epic." Milton is discussed on pp. 25–26 *passim.*]

147 PATTISON, Bruce. *Music and Poetry of the English Renaissance.* London: Methuen, 1948, 1970.†

148 POPKIN, Richard H. *The History of Scepticism from Erasmus to Descartes.* New York: Humanities Press, 1964. [Torchbook]†

148A POWELL, Chilton L. *English Domestic Relations, 1487–1653.* New York: Columbia Univ. Press, 1917.

149 QUINONES, Ricardo J. *The Renaissance Discovery of Time.* Cambridge: Harvard Univ. Press, 1972. [Milton is discussed in Ch. 11, pp. 444–493.]

150 RHYS, Hedley Howell, ed. *Seventeenth Century Science and the Arts.* Princeton: Princeton Univ. Press, 1961. [Lectures by Stephen Toulmin, Douglas Bush, James S. Ackerman, and Claude V. Palisca on science in relation to the arts: literature, visual art, and music.]

151 ROSENMEYER, Thomas G. *The Green Cabinet: Theocritus and the European Pastoral Tradition.* Berkeley, Los Angeles, London: Univ. of Calif. Press, 1969. [California]†

152 SAMUEL, Irene, and CAVALCHINI, Mariella. *Tasso's Discourses on the Heroic Poem.* Oxford: Clarendon Press, 1972. [A translation with notes and an introduction.]

153 SASEK, Lawrence. *The Literary Temper of the English Puritans.* Baton Rouge: Louisiana State Univ. Press, 1961.

154 SCHOLES, Percy A. *The Puritans and Music in England and New England.* London: Oxford Univ. Press, 1934.

155 SCHÜCKING, Levin L. *The Puritan Family: A Social Study from the Literary Sources.* Trans. Brian Battershaw. London: Routledge & Kegan Paul, 1969. [The German original first appeared in 1929.]

156 SEATON, Ethel. *Literary Relations of England and Scandinavia in the Seventeenth Century.* Oxford: Clarendon Press, 1935.

157 SEAVER, Paul S. *The Puritan Lectureships: The Politics of Religious Dissent.* Stanford: Stanford Univ. Press, 1970.

158 SELLS, A. Lytton. *The Paradise of Travellers: The Italian Influence on Englishmen in the Seventeenth Century.* Bloomington: Indiana Univ. Press, 1964.

11

USEFUL BACKGROUND STUDIES

159 SEZNEC, Jean. *The Survival of the Pagan Gods: The Mythological Tradition and Its Place in Renaissance Humanism and Art.* Trans. Barbara F. Sessions. New York: Pantheon, 1953. [Torchbook, also Princeton]†

160 SHUMAKER, Wayne. *The Occult Sciences in the Renaissance: A Study in Intellectual Patterns.* Berkeley, Los Angeles, London: Univ. of Calif. Press, 1972. [Chapters on Astrology, Witchcraft, White Magic, Alchemy, and Hermes Trismegistus.]

161 SIMON, Ulrich. *Heaven in the Christian Tradition.* New York: Harper, 1958.

162 SLOAN, Thomas O. "The Crossing of Rhetoric and Poetry in the English Renaissance." *The Rhetoric of Renaissance Poetry from Wyatt to Milton.* Ed. Thomas O. Sloan and Raymond B. Waddington. Berkeley, Los Angeles, London: Univ. of Calif. Press, 1974, pp. 212–242.

163 SMITH, Hallett. "English Metrical Psalms in the Sixteenth Century and Their Literary Significance." *HLQ,* 9 (1946), 249–271.

164 SONNINO, Lee. *A Handbook of Sixteenth Century Rhetoric.* London: Routledge & Kegan Paul; New York: Barnes & Noble, 1968.

165 SPINGARN, Joel E., ed. *Critical Essays of the Seventeenth Century.* 3 vols. Oxford: Oxford Univ. Press. 1908–1909; Bloomington: Indiana Univ. Press, 1957.

166 SPINGARN, Joel E. *A History of Literary Criticism in the Renaissance.* New York: Harcourt, Brace and World, 1963. [A Harbinger paperback with an introduction by Bernard Weinberg.]†

167 STEADMAN, John M. *The Lamb and the Elephant: Ideal Imitation and the Context of Renaissance Allegory.* San Marino, Calif.: Huntington Library, 1974.

168 STEADMAN, John M. " 'Meaning' and 'Name' : Some Renaissance Interpretations of Urania." *Neuphilologische Mitteilungen,* 64 (1963), 209–232.

169 STONE, Lawrence. *The Causes of the English Revolution 1529–1642.* New York: Harper and Row, 1972.

170 STONE, Lawrence. *The Crisis of the Aristocracy.* Oxford: Clarendon Press, 1965. [Abridged edition: Oxford paperback, 1967.]†

171 STOYE, John Walter. *English Travellers Abroad, 1604–1667: Their Influence in English Society and Politics.* London: Cape, 1952.

172 SWEDENBERG, H. T., Jr. *The Theory of the Epic in England, 1650–1800.* Berkeley and Los Angeles: Univ. of Calif. Press, 1944.

173 SYPHER, Wylie. *Four Stages of Renaissance Style: Transformations in Art and Literature 1400–1700.* Garden City, N.Y.: Doubleday, 1955. [Anchor]†

173A THOMAS, Keith. *Religion and the Decline of Magic,* New York: Scribner's 1971.

174 TILLYARD, E. M. W. *The Elizabethan World Picture.* London: Chatto & Windus, 1943. [Vintage, Penguin]†

175 TILLYARD, E. M. W. *The English Epic and Its Background.* London: Chatto & Windus; New York: Barnes & Noble, 1954. [Galaxy]†

176 TREVELYAN, George Macaulay. *England under the Stuarts.* New York: Putnam, 1904.

177 TREVELYAN, George Macaulay. *English Social History: A Survey of Six Centuries, Chaucer to Queen Victoria.* London: Longmans, Green, 1944. [Chapters VIII and IX deal with the backgrounds of English life in Milton's time.]

USEFUL BACKGROUND STUDIES

178 TUVESON, Ernest Lee. *Millennium and Utopia: A Study in the Background of the Idea of Progress.* Berkeley and Los Angeles: Univ. of Calif. Press, 1949. [Harper Torchbook]†

179 VICKERS, Brian. *Classical Rhetoric in English Poetry.* London: Macmillan; New York: St. Martins, 1970.

180 WALKER, D. P. *The Ancient Theology: Studies in Christian Platonism From the Fifteenth to the Eighteenth Century.* Ithaca: Cornell Univ. Press, 1972.

181 WALKER, D. P. *The Decline of Hell: Seventeenth-Century Discussions of Eternal Torment.* Chicago: Univ. of Chicago Press, 1964.

182 WEBSTER, Charles, ed. *The Intellectual Revolution of the Seventeenth Century.* London and Boston: Routledge & Kegan Paul, 1974. [A selection of essays published previously in *Past and Present.*]

183 WEDGWOOD, Cecily Veronica. *A Coffin for King Charles: The Trial and Execution of Charles I.* New York: Macmillan, 1964.

184 WEDGWOOD, Cecily Veronica. *The King's Peace: 1637–1641.* London: Collins, 1955.

185 WEDGWOOD, Cecily Veronica. *The King's War: 1641–1647.* London: Collins, 1959.

186 WEDGWOOD, Cecily Veronica. *Poetry and Politics under the Stuarts.* Cambridge: Cambridge Univ. Press, 1960. [Ann Arbor]†

187 WEDGWOOD, Cecily Veronica. *Seventeenth-Century English Literature* London: Oxford Univ. Press, 1956. [Galaxy]†

188 WEIDHORN, Manfred. *Dreams in Seventeenth-Century Literature.* The Hague: Mouton, 1970. [Ch. VI discusses Milton's comments on dreams and his use of dreams in his poetry.]

189 WEINBERG, Bernard. *A History of Literary Criticism in the Italian Renaissance.* 2 vols. Chicago: Univ. of Chicago Press, 1961.

190 WENDELL, Barrett. *The Temper of the Seventeenth Century in English Literature.* New York: Scribner's, 1904. [Discusses Milton specifically, pp. 267-326.]

191 WESTFALL, Richard H. *Science and Religion in Seventeenth-Century England.* New Haven: Yale Univ. Press, 1958. [Ann Arbor]†

192 WHITEHEAD, Alfred North. *Science and the Modern World.* New York: Macmillan, 1925. [Free Press]† [See the chapters entitled "Science and Religion" and "The Century of Genius."]

193 WILEY, Margaret. *The Subtle Knot: Creative Scepticism in Seventeenth-Century England.* London: George Allen, 1952.

194 WILLEY, Basil. *The Seventeenth-Century Background: Studies in the Thought of the Age in Relation to Poetry and Religion.* London: Chatto & Windus, 1934. [Anchor]† [Reprinted, New York: Columbia Univ. Press, 1952. Contains chapters on Milton under headings "On Scriptural Interpretation" and "The Heroic Poem in a Scientific Age."]

195 WILLIAMSON, George. *The Senecan Amble: Prose Form from Bacon to Collier.* London: Faber & Faber, 1951. [Phoenix]†

196 WILLIAMSON, George. *Seventeenth-Century Contexts.* London: Faber & Faber, 1960.

13

197 WILSON, John F. *Pulpit in Parliament: Puritanism During the English Civil Wars 1640–1648.* Princeton: Princeton Univ. Press, 1969.

198 WIND, Edgar. *Pagan Mysteries in the Renaissance.* London: Faber & Faber, 1958. [Norton.]† [Renaissance Iconography. Discusses Orpheus, Apollo, and other mythological figures pertinent to Milton.]

199 WOLFE, Don M., ed. *Leveller Manifestoes of the Puritan Revolution.* New York and London: Nelson, 1944.

200 WOLFE, Don M. *Milton and His England.* Princeton: Princeton Univ. Press, 1971. [Illustrated.]

201 WOODHOUSE, A. S. P., ed. *Puritanism and Liberty, Being the Army Debates (1647–9) from the Clarke Manuscripts, with Supplementary Documents.* London: J. M. Dent, 1938.

202 YULE, George. *The Independents in the English Civil War.* Cambridge: Cambridge Univ. Press, 1958.

202A ZAGORIN, Perez. *The Court and the Country: The Beginning of the English Revolution.* London: Routledge & Kegan Paul, 1969; New York: Atheneum, 1970.

203 ZAGORIN, Perez. *A History of Political Thought in the English Revolution.* London: Routledge & Kegan Paul, 1954.

Editions Published in Milton's Lifetime

A chronological arrangement has been adopted for this section, with a few works published for the first time after Milton's death being included. For detailed bibliographical discussions of these editions see the introductions and notes in the Columbia edition of the complete works (**271**) and in the Yale Prose (**306**).

204 "An Epitaph on the admirable Dramaticke Poet, W. SHAKESPEARE." [Prefixed to the second folio of] *Mr. William Shakespeare Comedies, Histories, and Tragedies,* 1632.

205 [*Comus.*] *A Maske Presented at Ludlow Castle, 1634.* London: H. Robinson, 1637. [Henry Lawes' edition.]

206 *Justa Edovardo King, naufrago, ab amicis moerentibus, amoris & μνείας χάριν.* Cantabrigiæ: apud Thoman Buck, & Rogerum Daniel, celeberrimæ academiæ typographos, 1638. [The second part, which includes the first printing of *Lycidas,* has a special title page: *Obsequies to the Memorie of Mr. Edward King, Anno Dom. 1638.*]

207 *Of Reformation Touching Church-Discipline in England: And the Causes that hitherto have hindered it.* [London]: Thomas Underhill, 1641.

208 *Of Prelatical Episcopacy, and Whether it may be deduc'd from the Apostolical times by vertue of those Testimonies which are alleg'd to that purpose in some late Treatises; One whereof goes under the Name of Iames Archbishop of Armagh.* London: Thomas Underhill, 1641.

14

209 *Animadversions upon the Remonstrants Defense, against Smectymnuus.* London: Thomas Underhill, 1641.

210 *The Reason of Church-government urg'd against Prelaty.* London: John Rothwell, 1642.

211 *An Apology Against a Pamphlet called A Modest Confutation of the Animadversions upon the Remonstrant against Smectymnuus.* London: John Rothwell, 1642.

212 *Epitaphium Damonis.* [1642? Privately printed without name or date.]

213 *The Doctrine and Discipline of Divorce: Restor'd to the Good of Both Sexes, From the bondage of Canon Law, and other mistakes, to Christian freedom, guided by the Rule of Charity.* London: T. P. & M. S., 1643. [2nd edition, "revis'd and much augmented," 1644.]

214 *Of Education: To Master Samuel Hartlib.* [London: Thomas Underhill, 1644.]

215 *The Judgment of Martin Bucer, Concerning Divorce. Writt'n to Edward the sixt, in his second Book of the Kingdom of Christ. And now Englisht.* London: Matthew Simmons, 1644.

216 *Areopagitica; A Speech of Mr. John Milton For the Liberty of Unlicenc'd Printing, To the Parlament of England.* London, 1644.

217 *Colasterion: A Reply to A Nameless Answer Against the Doctrine and Discipline of Divorce.* [London], 1645.

218 *Tetrachordon: Expositions Upon The foure chief places in Scripture, which treat of Mariage, or nullities in Mariage.* London. 1645.

219 *Poems of Mr. John Milton, Both English and Latin, Compos'd at Several Times. Printed by His True Copies. The Songs were Set in Musick by Mr. Henry Lawes.* London: H. Moseley, 1645/6.

220 [Sonnet to Henry Lawes.] [Prefixed to] *Choice Psalmes, Put into Musick for Three Voices.* By Henry and William Lawes. London: H. Moseley, 1648.

221 *The Tenure of Kings and Magistrates.* London: Matthew Simmons, 1649. [2nd ed., 1650.]

222 "Observations on the Articles of Peace." [Appended to] *Articles Of Peace, made and concluded with the Irish Rebels, and Papists, by James Earle of Ormond, for and in behalfe of the late King, and by vertue of his Autoritie.* London: Matthew Simmons, 1649.

223 EIKONOKLASTES *in Answer to a Book Intitl'd* EIKON BASILIKE, *The Portraiture of his Sacred Majesty in His Solitudes and Sufferings.* London: Matthew Simmons, 1649. [2d edition, 1650.]

224 *Joannis Miltoni Angli Pro Populo Anglicano Defensio Contra Claudii Anonymi, aliàs Salmasii, Defensionem Regiam.* Londini: Typis Du Gardianis, 1651.

225 *Joannis Miltoni Angli Pro Populo Anglicano Defensio Secunda, Contra infamen libellum anonymum cui titulus, Regii sanguinis clamor ad cœlum adversus parricidas Anglicanos.* Londini: Typis Neucomianis, 1654.

226 *Joannis Miltoni Angli pro se Defensio contra Alexandrum Morum Ecclesiasten, Libelli famosi, cui titulus, Regii sanguinis clamor ad cœlum adversus Parricidas Anglicanos, authorem rectè dictum.* Londini: Typis Neucomianis, 1655. Reprinted, Hagae-Comitum: ex typographia A. Vlacq, 1655.

227 *The Cabinet-Council: Containing the Chief Arts of Empire, and Mysteries of State ... By ... Sir Walter Raleigh.* London: Thomas Newcomb for Thomas Johnson, 1658. [Published by Milton from a manuscript.]

15

228 *Considerations Touching The likeliest means to remove Hirelings out of the church. Wherin is also discoursed of Tithes, Church-fees, Church-revenues; and whether any maintenance of ministers can be settl'd by law.* London: L. Chapman, 1659.

229 *A Treatise of Civil Power in Ecclesiastical Causes: Shewing That it is not lawfull for any power on earth to compell in matters of Religion.* London: Tho. Newcomb, 1659.

230 *The Readie & Easie Way to Establish a Free Commonwealth, and the Excellence thereof Compar'd with The inconveniences and dangers of readmitting kingship in this nation.* London: Livewell Chapman, 1660. [2d edition, "revis'd and augmented," 1660.]

231 *Brief Notes Upon a late Sermon, titl'd, The Fear of God and the King; Preachd, and since Publishd, By Matthew Griffith, D. D. And Chaplain to the late King.* London, 1660.

232 *Paradise Lost. A Poem Written in Ten Books by John Milton.* London: Peter Parker, Robert Boulter, & Matthias Walker, 1667.

233 *Accedence Commenc't Grammar, Supply'd with Sufficient Rules, For the use of such as, Younger or Elder, are desirous, without more trouble than needs, to attain the Latin Tongue; the elder sort especially, with little teaching, and thir own industry.* London: S. Simmons, 1669.

234 *The History of Britain, That part especially now call'd England. From the first Traditional Beginning, continu'd to the Norman Conquest.* London: James Allestry, 1670.

235 *Paradise Regain'd. A Poem. In IV Books. To Which Is Added Samson Agonistes. The Author John Milton.* London: John Starkey, 1671.

236 *Joannis Miltoni Angli, Artis Logicae Plenior Institutio.* Londini: Impensis Spencer Hickman, 1672.

237 *Of True Religion, Hæresie, Schism, Toleration, and what best mean may be us'd against the growth of Popery.* London, 1673.

238 *Poems, &c. upon Several Occasions. By Mr. John Milton: Both English and Latin, &c. Composed at Several Times. With a Small Tractate of Education to Mr. Hartlib.* London: T. Dring, 1673.

239 *Joannis Miltoni Angli, Epistolarum Familiarum Liber Unus: Quibus Accesserunt, Ejusdem, jam olim in Collegio Adolescentis, Prolusiones Quaedam Oratoriae.* Londini: Brabazoni Aylmeri, 1674.

240 *A Declaration or Letters Patents of the Election of this present King of Poland John the III.* London: Brabazon Aylmer, 1674.

241 *Paradise Lost. A Poem in Twelve Books. The Author John Milton. The Second Edition Revised and Augmented by the Same Author.* London: S. Simmons, 1674.

242 *Literæ Pseudo-Senatûs Anglicani, Cromwellii, Reliquorumque Perduellium nomine ac jussu conscriptæ [London: Moses Pitt], 1676.*

243 *A Brief History of Moscovia, and of Other Less-Known Countries Lying Eastward of Russia as far as Cathay. Gather'd from the Writings of Several Eye-witnesses.* London: Brabazon Aylmer, 1682.

244 *Letters of State, Written by Mr. John Milton, to most of the Sovereign Princes and Republicks of Europe. From the Year 1649. till the Year 1659. To Which Is Added, an Account of His Life. Together with Several of His Poems.* London, 1694. [A translation of *Literae Pseudo-Senatus* (1676) by Edward Phillips with Phillips' *Life.* The sonnets to Cromwell, Fairfax, Vane, and Skinner are printed for the first time.]

245 *Joannis Miltoni Angli De Doctrina Christiana libri duo posthumi, quos ex schedis mauscriptis deprompsit et typis mandari primus curavit C. R. Sumner.* Cantabrigiae: Typis Academicis, 1825. [Discovered in 1823. Printed for the first time in 1825.]

246 HORWOOD, A. J., ed. *A Common-place Book of John Milton, and a Latin Essay and Latin Verses Presumed To Be by Milton.* (Camden Society, N. S., 16) Westminster: Camden Society, 1876. [Discovered by Horwood in 1874. Printed for the first time in 1876.] Reprinted by Johnson Reprint Corp.

247 *A Common-Place Book of John Milton. Reproduced by the Autotype Process from the Original Manuscript in the Possession of Sir Frederick J. U. Graham. . . . With an Introduction by A. J. Horwood.* London: (privately printed), 1876.

Facsimiles of Editions Published in Milton's Lifetime

This section lists facsimiles of the works cited in the immediately preceding section.

248 *Accidence.* Menston, England: Scolar Press, 1971. [Facsimile reprint of 1st edition, 1669.]

249 *Areopagitica.* London: Noël Douglas, 1927. [Facsimile of 1644 edition.]

250 *Areopagitica.* New York: Columbia Univ. Press for the Facsimile Text Society, 1927. [Facsimile reprint of 1644 edition.]

251 *Areopagitica* and *Of Education.* Menston, England: Scolar Press, 1968. [Facsimile reprint of London edition of 1644.]†

252 BROWNING, Oscar, ed. *Milton's Tractate on Education. A Facsimile Reprint from the Edition of 1673.* Cambridge: Cambridge Univ. Press, 1883.

253 *The Cambridge Manuscript of John Milton: Lycidas and Some of the Other Poems Reproduced from the Collotype Facsimile.* (With a bibliographical note by Frank A. Patterson.) New York: Columbia Univ. Press, 1933.

254 DARBISHIRE, Helen, ed. *The Manuscript of Milton's Paradise Lost Book I.* Oxford: Clarendon Press, 1931. [A collotype facsimile with transcript, introduction, and notes.]

255 *English Poems* and *Comus.* Menston, England: Scolar Press, 1968. [Facsimile reprint of 1645 edition, omitting the Latin poems.]

256 FLETCHER, Harris Francis, ed. *John Milton's Complete Poetical Works, Reproduced in Photographic Facisimile.* See **281.**

257 LIVINGSTON, L. S., ed. *Comus.* New York: Dodd, Mead, 1903. [Facsimile of 1637 edition.]

258 *Lycidas:* 1637–1645. Menston, England: Scolar Press, 1970.†

259 MASSON, David, ed. *Paradise Lost as Originally Published by John Milton, Being a Facsimile Reproduction of the First Edition.* London: Stock, 1877. Reprinted by Folcraft Library Editions, 1972.

260 *Milton's Poems 1645: Type-facsimile.* Oxford: Clarendon Press, 1924.

261 MOSSNER, Ernest C., ed. *Justa Edovardo King.* New York: Columbia Univ. Press for the Facsimile Text Society, 1939.

262 *Paradise Lost.* Menston, England: Scolar Press, 1968. [Facsimile reprint of 1st edition of 1667.]†

263 *Paradise Regained* and *Samson Agonistes.* Menston, England: Scolar Press, 1968. [Facsimile reprint of 1671 edition.]†

264 *Poems.* Menston, England: Scolar Press, 1970. [Reproduced in facsimile from the manuscript in Trinity College, Cambridge, with a transcript.]†

265 *Poems 1645, Lycidas 1638.* Menston, England: Scolar Press, 1970. [Facsimile reprints of 1st editions.]†

266 *Poems . . . 1645.* New York: Columbia Univ. Press for the Facsimile Text Society, 1927. [Reproduction of 1645 edition exclusive of the Latin poems.]

267 *Prose Works* 1641–1650. 3 vols. Menston, England: Scolar Press, 1967–1968. [Vol. I (1968) includes facsimile reprints of 1641–1642 editions of the antiprelatical pamphlets. Vol. II (1968) includes facsimiles of the 1644–45 editions of the divorce tracts, *Of Education,* and *Areopagitica.* Vol. III (1967) includes facsimile of 1650 (2d rev.) editions of *Tenure of Kings and Magistrates* and *Eikonoklastes.*]

Collected Editions

The Columbia edition (271) is the only complete collection of all of Milton's writings, published and unpublished. It contains translations of the Latin works on pages facing the text and textual collations, but no explanatory notes. The Yale edition of the prose (306), to be completed in eight volumes with translations only of the Latin, is fully annotated.

Poetry and Prose

268 HUGHES, Merrit Y., ed. *John Milton. Complete Poems and Major Prose.* New York: Odyssey Press, 1957.

269 MITFORD, John, ed. *The Works of John Milton in Verse and Prose, Printed from the Original Editions with a Life of the Author.* 8 vols. London: Pickering, 1841.

270 PATTERSON, Frank Allen, ed. *The Student's Milton, Being the Complete Poems of John Milton, with the Greater Part of His Prose Works, Now Printed in One Volume, Together with New Translations into English of His Italian, Latin and Greek Poems.* Rev. ed. New York: Crofts, 1933. [First published in 1930.]

271 PATTERSON, Frank Allen, gen. ed. *The Works of John Milton.* 18 vols. in 21. New York: Columbia Univ. Press, 1931–1938. [Standard modern edition. See **30** for index. For various volumes see individual titles.] Reprinted by Somerset Publishers.

Poetry

272 BEECHING. H. C., ed. *The Poetical Works of John Milton, Edited after the Original Texts.* Oxford: Clarendon Press, 1900.

273 BROWNE, R. C., ed. *English Poems by John Milton.* 2 vols. Oxford: Clarendon Press, 1894.

274 BRYDGES, Sir Edgerton, ed. *The Poetical Works of John Milton. . . . with Imaginative Illustrations by J. M. W. Turner.* 6 vols. London: J. Macrone, 1835. Reprinted by AMS.

275 BUSH, Douglas, ed. *The Complete Poetical Works of John Milton.* Boston: Houghton Mifflin, 1965; London: Oxford Univ. Press, 1966.

276 CAREY, John, and FOWLER, Alastair, eds. *The Poems of John Milton.* London: Longmans, Green, 1968.

277 COWPER, William, trans. *Latin and Italian Poems of Milton Translated into English Verse, and a Fragment of a Commentary on* Paradise Lost. Ed. W. Hayley. London: J. Johnson & R. H. Evans, 1808.

278 DARBISHIRE, Helen, ed. *The Poetical Works of John Milton.* 2 vols. Oxford: Clarendon Press, 1952–1955. [Reprinted with Latin poems edited by H. W. Garrod and Italian poems edited by John Purves. London and New York: Oxford Univ. Press 1958. Miss Darbishire undertakes to reconstruct the text according to Milton's intentions with regard to spelling, etc.]

279 *The English Poems of John Milton From the Edition of H. C. Beeching Together with an Introduction by Charles Williams, and a Reader's Guide to Milton Compiled by Walter Skeat.* (World's Classics.) Oxford: Oxford Univ. Press; London: Milford, 1940. Williams' Introduction is reprinted in **498.**

280 FLETCHER, Harris Francis, ed. *The Complete Poetical Works of John Milton.* (New Cambridge Edition.) Boston: Houghton Mifflin, 1941.

281 FLETCHER, Harris Francis, ed. *John Milton's Complete Poetical Works, Reproduced in Photographic Facsimile.* 4 vols. Urbana: Univ. of Illinois Press, 1943–1848. [Vol. I (1943) includes 1645 and 1673 editions of Minor Poems, fugitive printings, and manuscript copies. Vol. II (1945) includes first edition of *Paradise Lost,* plans and lists of epic subjects of the Trinity College Manuscript, and the manuscript of Book I. Vol. III (1948) includes second edition of *Paradise Lost.* Vol. IV (1948) includes 1671 edition of *Paradise Regained* and *Samson Agonistes.*]

282 GRIERSON, H. J. C., ed. *The Poems of John Milton.* 2 vols. London: Chatto & Windus, 1925.

283 HAYLEY, W., ed. *Milton's Life and Poetical Works with Notes by William Cowper. . . . With Adam, a Sacred Drama.* 4 vols. Chichester: printed by W. Mason for J. Johnson, London, 1810.

284 HUGHES, Merritt Y., ed. *Paradise Regained, the Minor Poems and Samson Agonistes. Complete and Arranged Chronologically.* New York: Odyssey Press; Garden City: Doubleday, 1937.

19

COLLECTED EDITIONS

285 KEIGHTLEY, T., ed. *The Poems of John Milton.* 2 vols. London: Chapman & Hall, 1859.

286 MASSON, David, ed. *The Poetical Works of John Milton.* 3 vols. New York and London: Macmillan, 1874. [Revised edition 1890; reprinted 1894, 1896.]

287 *The Poetical Works of John Milton.* 2 vols. London: Tonson, 1705.

288 *The Poetical Works of John Milton,* 2 vols. Birmingham: Baskerville, 1758 [Notable for its printing.]

289 *The Poetical Works of John Milton. With a Life of the Author, by William Hayley.* 3 vols. London: Boydel & Nicol, 1794–1797. [Illustrations by R. Westall.]

290 *The Poetical Works of John Milton; with Introductions by David Masson. . . . Biographical Sketch by Nathan Haskell Dole.* New York and Boston: Crowell (1892).

291 *The Poetical Works of Mr. John Milton. Containing Paradise Lost, Paradise Regain'd, Samson Agonistes, and His Poems on Several Occasions. Together with Explanatory Notes on Each Book of the Paradise Lost* [i.e., Hume's *Annotations,* 861], *and a Table Never before Printed.* London: J. Tonson 1695, [5 parts in 1 vol.; parts separately published 1688–1695.]

292 SHAWCROSS, John T., ed. *The Complete Poetry of John Milton.* Rev. ed. Garden City: Doubleday, 1971. [Anchor]† [A composite text according to Milton's practices as evidenced by all the originals, printed or in manuscript.]

293 TODD, H. J., ed. *The Poetical Works of John Milton, with Notes of Various Authors. To Which are added Illustrations, and Some Account of the Life and Writings of Milton. . . . Second edition, with considerable additions and with a Verbal Index to the whole of Milton's poetry.* 7 vols. London: J. Johnson, 1809. [First published, London: J. Johnson, 1801.] Reprinted by AMS.

294 VERITY, A. W., ed. *The Cambridge Milton for Schools.* 10 vols. (Pitt Press Series.) Cambridge: Cambridge Univ. Press, 1891–1896. [Revised edition of *Comus* added in 1909. Revised edition of *Paradise Lost* added in 1910.]

295 WARTON, Thomas, ed. *Poems upon Several Occasions, English, Italian and Latin, With Translations by John Milton. . . . With Notes Critical and Explanatory and Other Illustrations.* London: J. Dodsley, 1785.

296 WRIGHT, B. A., ed. *John Milton. Poems.* (Everyman's Library.) London: Dent; New York: Dutton, 1956. [Eclectic reconstruction of Milton's intentions, differing from Darbishire.]

297 WRIGHT, William Aldis, ed. *The Poetical Works of John Milton.* Cambridge: Cambridge Univ. Press, 1903. [Fully modernized in spelling and punctuation.]

Prose

298 *Areopagitica and Other Prose Works of John Milton.* (Everyman's Library.) London: Dent, 1927.

299 *A complete Collection of the Historical, Political, and Miscellaneous Works of John Milton, both English and Latin; with som Papers Never Before Publish'd.* Amsterdam [London: ed. by Toland], 1698.

300 HUGHES, Merritt Y., ed. *John Milton: Prose Selections.* New York: Odyssey Press, 1947.

301 MABBOTT, Thomas Ollive, and FRENCH, J. Milton, eds. (with translations by Nelson Glenn McCrea and others). *The Uncollected Writings of John Milton.* Vol. XVIII in the Columbia *Milton* **(271)**], 1938.

302 PATRICK, J. Max, ed. *The Prose of John Milton.* Garden City: Doubleday, 1967. [Anchor]† New York: New York Univ. Press; London: Univ. of London Press, 1968. [Hardcover edition.]

303 PATRIDES, C. A., ed. *John Milton: Selected Prose.* Baltimore: Penguin, 1974.

304 ST. JOHN, J. A., ed. *The Prose Works of John Milton.* (Bohn's Standard Library.) 5 vols. London: Bell [1848]–1881.

305 WALLACE, Malcolm W., ed. *Milton's Prose.* (World's Classics.). London: Oxford Univ. Press, 1925. [A selection. Frequently reprinted.]

306 WOLFE, Don M., gen. ed. *Complete Prose Works of John Milton.* [To be published in 8 vols.] New Haven: Yale Univ. Press, 1953–. [For names of special editors see Individual Prose Works.]
    Vol. I: 1624–1642. Ed. Don M. Wolfe, et al. 1953.
    Vol. II: 1643–1648. Ed. Ernest Sirluck. 1959.
    Vol. III: 1648–1649. Ed. Merritt Y. Hughes. 1962.
    Vol. IV: 1650–1655. Ed. Don M. Wolfe. 1966.
    Vol. V, Part I: 1648?–1671. Ed. French Fogle. 1971.
    Vol. V, Part II: 1649–1659. Ed. J. Max Patrick. 1971.
    Vol. VI: ca. 1658–ca. 1660. Ed. Maurice Kelley. 1973.
    Vol. VII: 1659–1660. Ed. Robert W. Ayers. Historical Introduction by Austin Woolrych. 1974.

307 *The Works of Mr. John Milton.* [London], 1697.

Important Editions of Individual Works

Minor Poems

308 BROOKS, Cleanth, and HARDY, John E., eds. *Poems of Mr. John Milton: the 1645 Edition with Essays in Analysis.* New York: Harcourt, Brace, 1951.

309 BURDEN, Dennis, ed. *The Shorter Poems of John Milton.* New York: Barnes & Noble; London: Heinemann, 1970.

310 CAREY, John, ed. *John Milton: Complete Shorter Poems.* London: Longman, 1971.† [Includes *SA* and *PR.*]

311 *Comus. A Mask by John Milton. . . . Printed from the Text of. . . Henry John Todd, with Selected and Original Anecdotes and Annotations, Biographical, Explanatory, Critical and Dramatic, with Splendid Embellishments.* London: Mathews & Leigh, 1808. [Issued as a supplement to the Cabinet; or Monthly Report of Polite Literature, Vol. V.]

312 ELLEDGE, Scott, ed. *Milton's Lycidas, Edited to Serve as an Introduction to Criticism*. New York and London: Harper and Row, 1966. [In addition to the text of *Lycidas* with extensive notes and commentary, contains poems from *Justa Edovardo King*, representative classical and Renaissance works in the tradition, and a bibliography.]

313 HONIGMANN, E. A. J., ed. *Milton's Sonnets*. London, Melbourne, Toronto: Macmillan; New York: St. Martin's, 1966. [The texts with an introduction and commentary.]

314 MACKELLAR, Walter, ed. *The Latin Poems of John Milton*. New Haven: Yale Univ. Press for Cornell Univ.; London: Milford, 1930. Reprinted by Somerset Publishers.

315 *Milton's Comus: A Masque, in Two Acts. . . . The Original Music by Handel and Arne, with Some Additions by Bishop and Kelly; the Overture by Cherubini, the Dances by M. Ware*. London: J. Miller, 1815.

316 *Milton's Comus, being the Bridgewater Manuscript, with Notes and a Short Family Memoir, by the Lady Alix Egerton*. London: Dent, 1910.

317 PRINCE, F. T., ed. *Milton: Comus and Other Poems*. London: Oxford Univ. Press, 1968. [The other poems are "On the Morning of Christ's Nativity," "On Time," "At a Solemn Music," "L'Allegro," "Il Penseroso," "Arcades," "Lycidas," and 19 sonnets.]

318 *The Shorter English Poems*, ed. Frank Allen Patterson; *The Italian Poems*, ed. and trans. Arthur Livingston; *The Latin and Greek Poems*, ed. W. P. Trent in collaboration with Thomas O. Mabbott, with a translation by Charles Knapp. Vol. I, Pt. 1 in the Columbia Milton (**271**), 1931.

319 SMART, John S., ed. *The Sonnets of Milton*. Glasgow: Maclehose, Jackson, 1921. Reprinted by Clarendon Press, 1966.†

320 SPROTT, S. E., ed. *John Milton: A Maske: The Earlier Versions*. Toronto and Buffalo: Univ. of Toronto Press, 1973.

321 TODD, Henry John, ed. *Comus. . . . With Notes Critical and Explanatory by Various Commentators, and with Preliminary Illustrations; To Which is Added a Copy of the Mask from a Manuscript Belonging to His Grace the Duke of Bridgewater*. Canterbury: W. Bristow, et al., 1798. [Incorporated into Todd's Poetical Works, **293**.]

322 VERITY, A. W., ed. *A Maske*. (Pitt Press Series.) Cambridge: Cambridge Univ. Press, 1909. [Added to Verity's *Cambridge Milton*, **294**.]

Paradise Lost

323 BENTLEY, Richard, ed. *Milton's Paradise Lost. A New Edition*. London: Jacob Tonson, et al., 1732. See **1202, 1206, 1557**. [Reprinted by AMS.]

324 FOWLER, Alastair, ed. *John Milton: Paradise Lost*. London: Longman, 1971.†

325 HUGHES, Merritt Y., ed. *Paradise Lost*. New York: Odyssey Press, 1935.

326 LOFFT, Capel, ed. *Paradise Lost. . . . Printed from the First and Second Editions Collated. The Original System of Orthography Restored; the Punctuation Corrected and Extended. With Various Readings: and Notes; Chiefly Rhythmical*. Bury St. Edmund's: J. Rackham, 1792.

327 NEWTON, Thomas, ed. *Paradise Lost. . . . A New Edition, With Notes of Various Authors.* 2 vols. London: J. & R. Tonson, & S. Draper, 1749. [Illustrations by Francis Hayman.]

328 *Paradise Lost. . . . The Fourth Edition, Adorn'd with Sculptures.* London: Printed by Miles Flescher for R. Bentley & J. Tonson, 1688. [Elaborate subscription edition with the first illustrations to the poem, most of them designed by J. B. de Medina.]

329 PATTERSON, Frank Allen, ed. *Paradise Lost.* Vol. II, Pts. 1 and 2 in the Columbia Milton (271), 1931.

330 VERITY, A. W., ed. *Paradise Lost.* Cambridge: Cambridge Univ. Press, 1921. [Reprinted with some changes from the revised edition of 1910; see 294.] Reprinted by Folcroft.

Paradise Regained

331 DUNSTER, Charles, ed. *Paradise Regained. . . . with Notes of Various Authors.* London: T. Cadell & W. Davies, 1795. [Revised and reprinted, London: G. Stafford, 1800.] Reprinted by Folcroft. See 1030.

332 NEWTON, Thomas, ed. *Paradise Regain'd. . . . To Which Is Added Samson Agonistes: and Poems upon Several Occasions. . . . With Notes of Various Authors.* London: J. & R. Tonson, & S. Draper, 1752.

333 PATTERSON, Frank Allen, ed. *Paradise Regained.* Vol. II, Pt. 2 in the Columbia Milton (271), 1931.

Samson Agonistes

334 PATTERSON, Frank Allen, ed. *Samson Agonistes.* Vol. I, Pt. 2 in the Columbia Milton (271), 1931.

335 PRINCE, F. T., ed. *Samson Agonistes.* London: Oxford Univ. Press, 1957, 1970.

336 VERITY, A. W., ed. *Samson Agonistes.* (Pitt Press Series.) Cambridge: Cambridge Univ. Press, 1951. [First published as part of Verity's *Cambridge Milton,* 1892.]

Prose Works

337 AINSWORTH, Oliver M., ed. *Milton on Education. The Tractate of Education with Supplementary Extracts from Other Writings of Milton.* New Haven: Yale Univ. Press, 1928. [Reprinted by AMS.]

338 ALLISON, William Talbot, ed. *The Tenure of Kings and Magistrates, by John Milton.* New York: Holt, 1911.

339 ARBER, Edward, ed. *Areopagitica, 24 November 1644. Preceded by Illustrative Documents.* (English Reprints, No. 1.) London: A. Murry, 1868. [Reprinted, 1869, 1895, 1903.]

IMPORTANT EDITIONS OF INDIVIDUAL WORKS

340 AYERS, Robert W., ed. *Brief Notes upon a Late Sermon.* In Vol. VII of the Yale Prose **(306)**, 1974.

341 AYERS, Robert W., ed. *The Readie and Easie Way.* [First and Second Editions, along with *A Letter to a Friend* (Oct. 20, 1659), *Proposals of Certain Expedients* (preface and notes by Maurice Kelley), and *The Present Means.*] In Vol. VII of the Yale Prose **(306)**, 1974.

342 AYRES, Harry Morgan, ed. *Of Prelatical Episcopacy; Animadversions . . . against Smectymnuus; The Reason of Church Government; An Apology against a Pamphlet.* Vol. III, Pt. 1 in the Columbia Milton **(271)**, 1931.

343 CLARK, Donald L., ed. *Familiar Letters.* With Masson's trans. In Vol. XII of the Columbia Milton **(271)**, 1936.

344 CLARK, Donald L., ed. *Prolusions.* With a trans. by Bromley Smith. In Vol. XII of the Columbia Milton **(271)**, 1936.

345 CLARK, Evert Mordecai, ed. *The Ready and Easy Way to Establish a Free Commonwealth, by John Milton.* New Haven: Yale Univ. Press, 1916.

346 COOLIDGE, Lowell W., ed. *Colasterion.* In Vol. II of the Yale Prose **(306)**, 1959.

347 COOLIDGE, Lowell W., ed. *Doctrine and Discipline of Divorce.* In Vol. II of the Yale Prose **(306)**, 1959.

348 DORIAN, Donald C., ed. *Of Education.* In Vol. II of the Yale Prose **(306)**, 1959.

349 FELLOWES, R., trans. *The Second Defence of the People of England.* Printed in *The Prose Works of John Milton.* Ed. R. W. Griswold. 2 vols. Philadelphia: Hooker, 1845, II, 477–527. [Reprinted in *The Prose Works of John Milton.* Ed. J. A. St. John. 5 vols. London: Bell (1848)–1881), I, 214–300.]

350 FOGLE, French, R., ed. *The History of Britain.* In Vol. V, Pt. I, of the Yale Prose **(306)**, 1971.

351 GILBERT, Allan H., ed. and trans. *Artis Logicae Plenior Institutio.* Vol. XI in the Columbia Milton **(271)**, 1935.

352 GRACE, William J., ed. *Considerations Touching the Likeliest Means. . . .* In Vol. VII of the Yale Prose **(306)**, 1974.

353 GRACE, William J., ed. *A Defense of the People of England,* trans. Donald Mackenzie. In Vol. IV of the Yale Prose **(306)**, 1966.

354 GRACE, William J., ed. *A Treatise of Civil Power.* In Vol. VII of the Yale Prose **(306)**, 1974.

355 HALE, Will Taliaferro, ed. *Of Reformation Touching Church Discipline in England, by John Milton.* New Haven: Yale Univ. Press, 1916.

356 HALES, J. W., ed. *Milton's Areopagitica.* Rev. ed. Oxford: Clarendon Press, 1881. [First published in 1866.]

357 HALLER, William, ed. *The Tenure of Kings and Magistrates; Eikonoklastes.* Vol. V in the Columbia Milton **(271)**, 1932.

358 HALLER, William, ed. *A Treatise of Civil Power; Considerations touching the Likeliest Means to Remove Hirelings out of the Church; A Letter to a Friend Concerning the Ruptures of the Commonwealth; The Present means, and Brief Delineation of a Free Commonwealth; The Readie and Easie Way to Establish a Free Commonwealth; Brief Notes upon a Late Sermon; Of True Religion, Heresie, Schism, Toleration; Articles of Peace; A Declaration of Letters.* Vol. VI in the Columbia Milton **(271)**, 1932.

24

IMPORTANT EDITIONS OF INDIVIDUAL WORKS

359 HANFORD, James Holly, and DUNN, Waldo Hilary, eds. *De Doctrina Christiana.* With the trans. of Charles R. Sumner. Vols. XIV–XVII in the Columbia Milton **(271)**, 1933–1934.

360 HAUG, Ralph A., ed. *Reason of Church-Government.* In Vol. I of the Yale Prose **(306)**, 1953.

361 HUGHES, Merritt Y., ed. *Eikonoklastes.* In Vol. III of the Yale Prose **(306)**, 1962.

362 HUGHES, Merritt Y., ed. *Observations upon the Articles of Peace.* In Vol. III of the Yale Prose **(306)**, 1962.

363 HUGHES, Merritt Y., ed. *The Tenure of Kings and Magistrates.* In Vol. III of the Yale Prose **(306)**, 1962.

364 JOCHUMS, Milford C., ed. *An Apology against a Pamphlet Called A Modest Confutation of the Animadversions upon the Remonstrant against Smectymnuus.* Urbana: Univ. of Illinois Press, 1950.

365 KELLEY, Maurice, ed. *Christian Doctrine,* trans. John Carey. In Vol. VI of the Yale Prose **(306)**, 1973.

366 KEYES, Clinton W., ed. *Joannis Miltoni Angli Pro Populo Anglicano Defensio.* With a trans. by Samuel Lee Wolff. Vol. VII in the Columbia Milton **(271)**, 1932.

367 KIRK, Rudolf, ed. *Animadversions.* In Vol. I of the Yale Prose **(306)**, 1953.

368 KRAPP, George Philip, ed. *The History of Britain; A Brief History of Moscovia.* Vol. X in the Columbia Milton **(271)**, 1932.

369 LEA, K. M., ed. *Areopagitica and Of Education.* Oxford: Clarendon Press, 1973.

370 MABBOTT, Thomas Ollive, ed. *English Correspondence.* In Vol. XII of the Columbia Milton **(271)**, 1936.

371 MABBOTT, Thomas Ollive, and FRENCH, J. Milton, eds. *The State Papers of John Milton.* Vol. XIII in the Columbia Milton **(271)**, 1937.

372 MABBOTT, Thomas Ollive, and MCCREA, Nelson G., eds. *An Early Prolusion and Miscellaneous Correspondence in Foreign Tongues.* In Vol. XII of the Columbia Milton **(271)**, 1936.

373 MABBOTT, Thomas Ollive, and MCCREA, Nelson G., eds. *Correspondence of Milton and Mylius.* In Vol. XII of the Columbia Milton **(271)**, 1936.

374 MCEUEN, Kathryn A., ed. *Prolusions.* With translations by Phyllis B. Tillyard. In Vol. I of the Yale Prose **(306)**, 1953.

375 MOHL, Ruth. ed. *Commonplace Book.* In Vol. I of the Yale Prose **(306)**, 1953.

376 PATRICK, J. Max, ed. *The Miltonic State Papers.* In Vol. V, Pt. II, of the Yale Prose **(306)**, 1971.

377 PATRICK, J. Max, ed. *Of Prelatical Episcopacy.* In Vol. I of the Yale Prose **(306)**, 1953.

378 POWELL, Chilton Latham, and HALLER, William, eds. *The Judgment of Martin Bucer; Tetrachordon; Colasterion; Of Education; Areopagitica.* Vol. IV in the Columbia Milton **(271)**, 1931.

379 POWELL, Chilton Latham, and PATTERSON, Frank Allen, eds. *The Doctrine and Discipline of Divorce.* Vol. III, Pt. 2 in the Columbia Milton **(271)**, 1931.

380 ROBERTS, Donald A., ed. *A Second Defense of the English People,* trans. Helen North. In Vol. IV of the Yale Prose **(306)**, 1966.

381 SIRLUCK, Ernest, ed. *Areopagitica.* In Vol. II of the Yale Prose (306), 1959.

382 STRITTMATTER, Eugene J., ed. *Joannis Miltoni Angli Pro Populo Anglicano Defensio Secunda.* With the trans. of George Burnett, London, 1809, rev. by Moses Hadas. Vol. VIII in the Columbia Milton (271), 1933.

383 STRITTMATTER, Eugene J., ed. *Joannis Miltoni Angli Pro Se Defensio contra Alexandrum Morum Ecclesiasten.* With the trans. of George Burnett, London, 1809, rev. by Moses Hadas. Vol. IX in the Columbia Milton (271), 1933.

384 SUMNER, Charles R., trans. *A Treatise of Christian Doctrine, Compiled from the Holy Scriptures Alone by John Milton.* Cambridge: Cambridge Univ. Press; Boston: Cummings, 1825. [Revised by Sumner for Bohn edition (304), 1848–1853.]

385 SVENDSEN, Kester, ed. *Pro Se Defensio,* trans. Paul W. Blackford. In Vol. IV of the Yale Prose (306), 1966.

386 TAFT, Frederick L., ed. *An Apology against a Pamphlet.* In Vol. I of the Yale Prose (306), 1953.

387 TILLYARD, Phyllis B., tr. *Private Correspondence and Academic Exercises, Translated from the Latin . . . with an Introduction and Commentary by E. M. W. Tillyard.* Cambridge: Cambridge Univ. Press, 1932.

388 TURNER, W. Arthur, and TURNER, Alberta T., eds. and trans. *Private Correspondence.* In Vols. I, II, IV, VII of the Yale Prose (306), 1953, 1959, 1966, 1974.

389 WILLIAMS, Arnold, ed. *The Judgment of Martin Bucer.* In Vol. II of the Yale Prose (306), 1959.

390 WILLIAMS, Arnold, ed. *Tetrachordon.* In Vol. II of the Yale Prose (306), 1959.

391 WOLFE, Don M., and ALFRED, William, eds. *Of Reformation.* In Vol. I of the Yale Prose (306), 1953.

Biographies

The most comprehensive treatment of Milton's life and times is still that of David Masson (408). The two-volume biography by William Riley Parker (410) includes data discovered since Masson and contains, in volume 2, a wide range of useful bibliographical information. French's *Life Records* (399) reprints the documents in a year-by-year survey of the events on which they have a bearing. The introductions to the Yale editions (306) contain full discussions of the backgrounds and circumstances of the prose works. A few short lives are listed here as convenient and accessible, or because they embody judgments which are still at issue or are of importance historically. Handbooks and surveys of Milton's literary career will be found under other headings.

392 BAILEY, John C. *Milton.* (Home University Library.) London: Oxford Univ. Press; New York: Williams & Norgate, 1915.

393 BELLOC, Hilaire. *Milton.* London: Cassell; Philadelphia: Lippincott, 1935.

394 BRYDGES, Sir Egerton. *Milton.* London: J. Macrone [1835].

395 BUSH, Douglas. *John Milton: A Sketch of his Life and Writings.* New York: Macmillan, 1964 [Collier, 1967]†

BIOGRAPHIES

396 DARBISHIRE, Helen, ed. *The Early Lives of Milton.* London: Constable, 1932. [John Aubrey, the anonymous biographer (John Phillips?), Anthony Wood, Edward Phillips, John Toland, and Jonathan Richardson.]

397 DIEKHOFF, John S., ed. *Milton on Himself: Milton's Utterances upon Himself and His Works.* New York: Oxford Univ. Press, 1939. Rev. ed. New York: Humanities Press, 1965.

398 FLETCHER, Harris F. *The Intellectual Development of John Milton.* Urbana: Univ. of Illinois Press, 1956–. Vol. I: *The Institution to 1625: From the Beginnings Through Grammar School.* 1956. Vol. II: *The Cambridge University Period, 1625–32.* 1961.

399 FRENCH, J. Milton, ed. *The Life Records of John Milton* 5 vols. New Brunswick, N.J.: Rutgers Univ. Press, 1949–1958. [Reprinted New York: Gordian, 1966.]

400 HANFORD, James Holly. *John Milton, Englishman.* New York: Crown, 1949; London: Victor Gollancz, 1950. [Crown]† [Reprinted Cleveland: Western Reserve, 1966.]

401 HANFORD, James Holly. *John Milton: Poet and Humanist.* Cleveland: Western Reserve Univ. Press, 1966. [A collection of previously published essays. For the titles of the essays see **526.**]

402 HAYLEY, William. *The Life of Milton* (2d ed., 1796). A facsimile reproduction with an introduction by J. A. Wittreich, Jr. Gainesville, Florida: Scholars' Facsimiles and Reprints, 1970.

403 IVIMEY, Joseph. *John Milton, His Life and Times, Religious and Political Opinions with an Appendix Containing Animadversions upon Dr. Johnson's* Life of Milton. London: E. Wilson, 1833.

404 JOHNSON, Samuel. "Life of Milton." *The Works of the Most Eminent English Poets, with Prefaces, Biographical and Critical.* London, 1779–1781.

405 KEIGHTLEY, Thomas. *An Account of the Life, Opinions and Writings of John Milton.* London: Chapman & Hall, 1855. [Reprinted, 1959.]

406 MACAULAY, Rose. *Milton.* London: Duckworth, 1933. [Collier, 1962]†

407 MCLAUGHLIN, Elizabeth T. "Milton and Thomas Ellwood." *Milton Newsletter,* 1 (1967), 17–28. [See **412, 413.**]

408 *MASSON, David. The Life of John Milton: Narrated in Connexion with the Political, Ecclesiastical, and Literary History of His Time.* 7 vols. Cambridge and London: Macmillan, 1859–1894. *[Vol. I revised in 1881. Index added 1894. Reprinted, New York: Peter Smith, 1946, 1965.]*

409 MORAND, Paul P. *De Comus à Satan: L'oeuvre Poétique de John Milton expliquée par sa vie.* Paris: Didier, 1939.

410 PARKER, William Riley. *Milton: A Biography.* 2 vols. Oxford: Clarendon Press, 1968.

411 PARSONS, Edward S., ed. "The Earliest Life of Milton." *EHR,* 17 (1902), 95–110. [Reprinted, Colorado Springs: Colarado College, 1903; and Boston: Lockwood, 1911.]

412 PATRICK, J. Max. "The Influence of Thomas Ellwood Upon Milton's Epics." *Essays in History and Literature.* Ed. Heinz Bluhm. Chicago: Newberry Library, 1965, pp. 119–132. [See **407, 413.**]

413 PATRICK, J. Max. "Milton and Thomas Ellwood: A Reconsideration." *Milton N,* 2 (1968), 2–4.

414 PATTISON, Mark. *Milton.* (English Men of Letters Series.) London: Macmillan, 1879, [Often reprinted.]

415 RAYMOND, Dora B. *Oliver's Secretary: John Milton in an Era of Revolt.* New York: Minton, Balch, 1932.

416 SAILLENS, Emile. *John Milton, poète combattant.* [Paris]: Gallimard, 1959. [Reprinted as *John Milton: Man, Poet, Polemicist.* New York: Barnes & Noble, 1964.]

417 STERN, Alfred. *Milton und seine Zeit.* 2 vols. Leipzig: Duncker & Humblot, 1877–1879.

418 TILLYARD, E. M. W. *Milton.* Rev. ed. London: Chatto & Windus, 1966. [Collier, 1967.]† [Chs. III and IV of Part III are reprinted in **499.**]

419 TODD, Henry John. "Some Account of the Life and Writings of John Milton." [Vol. I of Todd's variorum edition **293,** pp. 3–184.]

420 TRENT, William P. *John Milton: a Short Study of His Life and Works.* New York: Macmillan, 1899.

Biographical Studies

421 ADEMOLLO, A. *La Leonora di Milton e di Clemente* IX. Milano: Ricordi [1885].

422 ALLODOLI, Ettore. *Giovanni Milton e l'Italia.* Prato: C. & G. Spighi, 1907.

422A BARUCH, Franklin B. "Milton's Blindness: The Conscious and Unconscious Patterns of Autobiography." *ELH,* 42 (1975), 26–37.

423 BRENNECKE, Ernest, Jr. *John Milton the Elder and His Music.* New York: Columbia Univ. Press, 1938. [Reprinted by Octagon Books, 1973.]

424 BROWN, Eleanor G. *Milton's Blindness.* New York: Columbia Univ. Press; London: Milford, 1934.

425 BUSH, Douglas. "The Critical Significance of Biographical Evidence: John Milton." *English Institute Essays 1946,* pp. 5–19.

426 CHEW, Beverly. "Portraits of Milton." *Bibliographer,* 2 (1903), 92–101.

427 CLARK, Donald L. *John Milton at St. Paul's School, a Study of Ancient Rhetoric in English Renaissance Education.* New York: Columbia Univ. Press, 1948, 1964.

428 CLAVERING, Rose, and SHAWCROSS, John T. "Anne Milton and the Milton Residences." *JEGP,* 59 (1960), 680–690.

429 CLAVERING, Rose, and SHAWCROSS, John T. "Milton's European Itinerary and His Return Home." *SEL,* 5 (1965), 49–59. [Re-examination of Milton's travel plans and of the reasons for giving up the excursion to Sicily and Greece.]

430 DORIAN, Donald C. *The English Diodatis. A History of Charles Diodati's Family and His Friendship with Milton.* New Brunswick, N.J.: Rutgers Univ. Press, 1950.

431 ELTON, William. "New Light on Milton's Amanuensis." *HLQ,* 26 (1963), 383–384.

BIOGRAPHICAL STUDIES

432 EVANS, Willa M. *Henry Lawes: Musician and Friend of Poets.* (MLA Revolving Fund Series, 11.) New York: Modern Language Association of America; London: Oxford Univ. Press, 1941.

433 FRENCH, J. Milton. "The Autographs of John Milton." *ELH,* 4 (1937), 300–330.

434 FRENCH, J. Milton. *Milton in Chancery: New Chapters in the Lives of the Poet and His Father.* (MLA Monograph Series, 10.) New York: Modern Language Association of America; London: Milford, Oxford Univ. Press, 1939.

435 FRENCH, J. Milton. "The Powell-Milton Bond." *Harvard Studies and Notes,* 20 (1938), 61–73.

436 FRENCH, J. Milton. "The Reliability of Anthony Wood and Milton's Oxford M.A." *PMLA,* 75 (1960), 22–30.

437 GILBERT, Allan H. "The Cambridge Manuscript and Milton's Plans for an Epic." *SP,* 16 (1919), 172–176.

438 GILBERT, Allan H. "Milton and Galileo." *SP,* 19 (1922), 152–185.

439 GODWIN, William. *Lives of Edward and John Philips, Nephews and Pupils of Milton. Including Various Particulars of the Literary and Poetical History of Their Times. . . . To Which are Added, I. Collections for the Life of Milton. By John Aubrey, FRS. Printed from the Manuscript Copy in the Ashmolean Museum at Oxford. II. The Life of Milton. By Edward Philips. Printed in the Year 1694.* London: Longman, Hurst, Rees, Orme, & Brown, 1815.

440 GRANNIS, Ruth S. "The Beverley Chew Collection of Milton Portraits." *BNYPL,* 30 (1926), 3–6.

441 GRAVESON, S. ed. *The History and Life of Thomas Ellwood, Written by His Own Hand, with Extracts from Joseph Wyeth's Supplement, Appendices, and Biographical Notes.* London: Headley Bros., 1906. [Ellwood's autobiography was first published in 1714.]

442 HALES, John W. *Folia Literaria.* New York: Macmillan, 1893. ["Milton's 'Macbeth'," pp. 198–219; "Milton and Gray's Inn Walks," pp. 220–230; "Milton Notes," pp. 231–245.]

443 HAMILTON, W. Douglas. *Original Papers Illustrative of the Life and Writings of John Milton, including Sixteen Letters of State Written by Him Now First Published from Manuscripts in the State Paper Office. With an Appendix of Documents Relating to His Connection with the Powell Family.* London: Camden Society, 1859. [Reprinted by AMS.]

444 HANFORD, James Holly. "The Chronology of Milton's Private Studies." *PMLA,* 36 (1921), 251–314. [Reprinted in **401**.]

445 HANFORD, James Holly. "John Milton Forswears Physic." *Bulletin of the Medical Library Association,* 32 (1944), 23–34.

446 HANFORD, James Holly. "Milton in Italy." *AnM,* 5 (1964), 49–63.

447 HANFORD, James Holly. "The Youth of Milton. An Interpretation of His Early Development." *Studies in Shakespeare, Milton, and Donne.* New York: Macmillan, 1925, pp. 89–163. [Reprinted in **401**.]

447A HILL, John Spencer. "Poet-Priest: Vocational Tension in Milton's Early Development." *Milton Studies VIII* (1975), 41–69.

448 HONE, Ralph E. "New Light on the Milton-Phillips Family Relationship." *HLQ,* 22 (1958), 63–75.

29

BIOGRAPHICAL STUDIES

449 HUNTER, Joseph. *Milton. A Sheaf of Gleanings after His Biographers and Annotators: I. Genealogical Investigation; II. Notes on Some of His Poems.* London: J. R. Smith, 1850.

450 HUNTER, William B., Jr. "John Milton: Autobiographer." *Milton Quarterly,* 8 (1974), 100–104.

451 HUNTER, William B., Jr. "Some Speculations on the Nature of Milton's Blindness." *JHM,* 17 (1962), 333–341.

452 HUTTAR, Charles A. "Samson's Identity Crisis and Milton's." *Imagination and the Spirit: Essays in Literature and the Christian Faith presented to Clyde S. Kilby.* Ed. Charles A. Huttar. Grand Rapids, Mich.: William B. Eerdmans, 1971, pp. 101–157.

453 LILJEGREN, S. B. "Milton at Florence." *Neophil, 43 (1959), 133–137.*

454 LILJEGREN, S. B. *Studies in Milton.* Land: Gleerup, 1919. [Two main parts: "Milton and Galileo" and "Milton and the Pamela Prayer."]

455 MARSH, John Fitchett. *Papers Connected with the Affairs of Milton and His Family.* (Chetham Society Miscellanies, I.) Manchester: Chetham Society, 1851.

456 MARTIN, Burns. "The Date of Milton's First Marriage." *SP,* 25 (1928), 457–461.

457 MARTIN, John Rupert. "The Milton Portrait: Some Addenda." *PULC,* 24 (1963), 168–173.

458 MARTIN, John Rupert. *The Portrait of John Milton at Princeton, and Its Place in Milton Iconography.* Princeton: Princeton Univ. Press, 1961.

459 MASSON, David. [On Milton's Youth]. *North British Review,* 16 (1852), 155–176. [Reprinted in *Essays, Biographical and Critical: Chiefly on English Poets.* Cambridge: Macmillan, 1856, pp. 37–52.]

460 MORAND, Paul P. *The Effects of His Political Life upon John Milton.* Paris: Didier, 1939.

461 PARKER, William R. "The Anonymous Life of Milton." *TLS,* Sept. 13, 1957, 547.

462 PARKER, William R. "John Milton, Scrivener, 1590–1632." *MLN,* 59 (1944), 532–537.

463 PARKER, William R. "Wood's Life of Milton: Its Sources and Significance." *PBSA,* 52 (1958), 1–22.

464 READ, Allen Walker. "The Disinterment of Milton's Remains." *PMLA,* 45 (1930), 1050–1068.

465 ROSENBERG, D. M. "Theme and Structure in Milton's Autobiographies." *Genre,* 2 (1969), 314–325.

466 SHAWCROSS, John T. "The Chronology of Milton's Major Poems." *PMLA,* 76 (1961), 345–358. [See **469, 1239.**]

467 SHAWCROSS, John T. "Milton's Decision to Become a Poet." *MLQ,* 24 (1963), 21–30.

468 SHAWCROSS, John T. "Speculations on the Dating of the Trinity MS. of Milton's Poems." *MLN,* 75 (1960), 11–17.

469 SIRLUCK, Ernest. "Milton's Idle Right Hand." *JEGP,* 60 (1961), 749–785. [Effects of Milton's first marriage and later of his blindness on his poetic inspiration. Contains an appendix entitled "Some Recent Suggested Changes in the Chronology of Milton's Poem," pp. 773–785, in which he disputes W. R. Parker's early dating of *SA.* The appendix also discusses the dating of Sonnet VII and *Ad Patrem.*]

470 STEVENS, David H. *Milton Papers.* Chicago: Univ. of Chicago Press, 1927. [Chapters: "Some Real Estate Transactions of John Milton and his Father." "Mary Powell's Lost Dowry." "The Bridgewater Manuscript of *Comus.*" "The Stage Version of *Comus.*" "The Will of Edward King." Appendix: "Four Milton Deeds."]

471 VISIAK, E. H. *Milton Agonistes: a Metaphysical Criticism.* London: Philpot, 1923. [Psychological study.]

472 WOLFE, Don M. *Milton in the Puritan Revolution.* New York and London: Nelson, 1941. [Reprinted by Humanities Press, 1963.]

473 WRIGHT, B. A. "The Alleged Falsehoods in Milton's Account of His Continental Tour." *MLR,* 28 (1933), 308–314.

474 WRIGHT, B. A. "Milton's First Marriage." *MLR,* 26 (1931), 383–400; 27 (1932), 6–23.

Collections of Essays

Many of the individual essays in these collections are cited elsewhere under the appropriate headings.

475 AMES, Percy W., ed. *Milton Memorial Lectures, 1908.* London: Oxford Univ. Press, 1909. [Lectures on various topics by G. C. Williamson, W. H. Hadow, E. H. Coleridge, W. E. A. Axon, E. H. Pember, E. B. Saintsbury, H. G. Rosedale, E. Dowden, E. Brasbrook, and A. Vamberg.]

476 BARKER, Arthur E., ed. *Milton: Modern Essays in Criticism.* New York: Oxford Univ. Press, 1965. [Galaxy Book, 1965]†

477 BLONDEL, Jacques, ed. *Le Paradis Perdu 1667–1967.* Paris: Minard, 1967. [A tercentenary collection of essays in French by Pierre Brunel, Jacques Blondel, René Lejosne, Paul Rozenberg, Raymond Tschum, Mario Praz, Jean Gillet, Max Milner, Jacques Seebacher, Robert Couffignal, and Helen Gardner (trans. from *A. Reading of PL*).]

478 *Christ's College Magazine,* 23 (1908), No. 68. [Milton tercentenary number. Contains contributions by Austin Dobson, C. R. Fay, John W. Hales, J. W. Mackail, J. W. Peile, J. C. Sayle, W. W. Skeat, and others.]

479 *Critical Essays on Milton from ELH.* Baltimore, London: Johns Hopkins Press, 1969.

480 CRUMP, Galbraith M., ed. *Twentieth-Century Interpretations of Samson Agonistes: A Collection of Critical Essays.* Englewood Cliffs, N. J.: Prentice-Hall, 1968.

481 DYSON, A. E., and LOVELOCK, Julian, eds. *Milton: Paradise Lost: A Casebook.* London: Macmillan, 1973.

COLLECTIONS OF ESSAYS

482 EMMA, Ronald D., and SHAWCROSS, John T., eds. *Language and Style in Milton: A Symposium in Honor of the Tercentenary of Paradise Lost.* New York: Ungar, 1967.

483 FIORE, Amadeus P., O. F. M., ed. *Th' Upright Heart and Pure: Essays on John Milton Commemorating the Tercentenary of the Publication of Paradise Lost.* Pittsburgh: Duquesne Univ. Press; Louvain: E. Nauwelaerts, 1967.

484 GRIFFITH, Philip M., and ZIMMERMAN, Lester F., eds. *Papers on Milton.* Tulsa: Univ. of Tulsa, 1969.

485 HONE, Ralph E., ed. *John Milton's Samson Agonistes: The Poem and Materials for Analysis.* San Francisco: Chandler, 1966.

486 KERMODE, Frank, ed. *The Living Milton: Essays by Various Hands.* London: Routledge & Kegan Paul, 1960, 1973.†

487 KRANIDAS, Thomas, ed. *New Essays on Paradise Lost.* Berkeley and Los Angeles: Univ. of California Press, 1969, 1971.†

488 LIEB, Michael, and SHAWCROSS, John T., eds. *Achievements of the Left Hand: Essays on the Prose of John Milton.* Amherst: Univ. of Mass. Press, 1974.

489 MARTZ, Louis L., ed. *Milton: A Collection of Critical Essays.* Englewood Cliffs, N. J.: Prentice-Hall, 1966.†

490 *Milton Studies in Honor of Harris Francis Fletcher.* Urbana: Univ. of Illinois Press, 1961. [A reprint in hardback of the October 1961 issue of *JEGP*. Repaged.]

491 PATRIDES, C. A., ed. *Approaches to Paradise Lost: The York Tercentenary Lectures.* Toronto: Univ. of Toronto Press, 1968.

492 PATRIDES, C. A., ed. *Milton's Epic Poetry: Essays on Paradise Lost and Paradise Regained.* Baltimore: Penguin, 1967.†

493 PATRIDES, C. A., ed. *Milton's Lycidas: The Tradition and the Poem.* New York: Holt, Rinehart, and Winston, 1961.† [Contains the text of *Lycidas* and *Epitaphium Damonis* (Latin and English translation), an annotated reading list, and critical essays by James Holly Hanford, Samuel Johnson, E. M. W. Tillyard, John Crowe Ransom, Paul Elmer More, Josephine Miles, David Daiches, Richard P. Adams, Wayne Shumaker, Cleanth Brooks and John Edward Hardy, F. T. Prince, Rosemond Tuve, Northrop Frye, and M. H. Abrams.]

494 RAJAN, Balachandra, ed. *Paradise Lost: A Tercentenary Tribute.* Toronto: Univ. of Toronto Press, 1969. [Papers given at the Conference on the Tercentenary of *Paradise Lost,* University of Western Ontario, October, 1967.]

495 RAJAN, Balachandra, ed. *The Prison and the Pinnacle.* Toronto and Buffalo: Univ. of Toronto Press, 1973. [Papers to commemorate the Tercentenary of *Paradise Regained* and *Samon Agonistes,* read at the University of Western Ontario, March-April 1971.]

496 RUDRUM, Alan, ed. *Milton: Modern Judgements.* London: Macmillan, 1969; London: Macmillan; Nashville, Tenn.: Aurora, 1970.†

497 STEIN, Arnold, ed. *On Milton's Poetry: A Selection of Modern Studies.* Greenwich, Conn.: Fawcett, 1970.

498 SUMMERS, Joseph H., ed. *The Lyric and Dramatic Milton: Selected Papers from the English Institute.* New York and London: Columbia Univ. Press, 1965.

499 THORPE, James, ed. *Milton Criticism: Selections from Four Centuries.* New York: Holt, Rinehart and Winston, 1950; London: Routledge & Kegan Paul, 1951. [Collier, 1969]†

500 WITTREICH, Joseph Anthony, Jr., ed. *Calm of Mind:·Tercentenary Essays on Paradise Regained and Samson Agonistes in Honor of John S. Diekhoff.* Cleveland and London: The Press of Case Western Reserve Univ., 1971.

500A WITTREICH, Joseph Anthony, Jr., ed. *Milton and the Line of Vision.* Madison: Univ. of Wisconsin Press, 1975. [A collection of eight essays which cumulatively attempt to place Milton within a tradition of prophecy.]

General Criticism and Interpretation

Since many of the items listed under *Special Topics* range widely over a number of individual works, anyone interested in broad coverage would do well to consult *Special Topics* as well as this section.

501 ALLEN, Don Cameron. *The Harmonious Vision: Studies in Milton's Poetry.* Baltimore: Johns Hopkins Press, 1954, 1970. [Chapters on: " 'L'Allegro' and 'Il Penseroso'." " 'On the Morning of Christ's Nativity' and *A Mask.*" "The *Epicedia* and 'Lycidas'." "Despair and *Samson Agonistes.*" "The Visual Image in *Paradise Lost.*" "*Paradise Regained.*" "The Descent to Light: Basic Metaphor in *Paradise Lost*" appears only in the 1970 edition.]

502 ARNOLD, Matthew. "Milton." *Essays in Criticism. Second Series.* London and New York: Macmillan, 1888.

503 BAGEHOT, Walter. "John Milton." *Literary Studies.* 2 vols. London: Longmans, Green, 1879, I, 173–220.

504 BARKER, Arthur E. "Calm Regained Through Passion Spent: The Conclusion of the Miltonic Effort." *The Prison and the Pinnacle,* ed. B. Rajan **(495)** pp. 3–48.

505 BRISMAN, Leslie. *Milton's Poetry of Choice and Its Romantic Heirs.* Ithaca and London: Cornell Univ. Press, 1973.

506 BROADBENT, John. *John Milton: Introductions.* Cambridge: Cambridge Univ. Press, 1973.

507 BUDICK, Sanford. "Milton's Epic Reclamations." *Poetry of Civilization: Mythopoeic Displacement in the Verse of Milton, Dryden, Pope, and Johnson.* New Haven and London: Yale Univ. Press, 1974, pp. 41–80.

508 BUSH, Douglas. "John Milton." *Explication as Criticism: Selected Papers from the English Institute 1941–1952.* Ed. W. K. Wimsatt, Jr. New York: Columbia Univ. Press, 1963, pp. 131–145.

509 BUSH, Douglas. "Milton." *English Literature in the Earlier Seventeenth Century: 1600–1660.* 2d ed. Oxford: Clarendon Press, 1962, pp. 337–420. [First published in 1945.] Vol. v in *The Oxford History of English Literature.* Ed. F. P. Wilson and Bonamy Dobree. [To be published in] 12 vols. Oxford: Oxford Univ. Press, 1945–.

510 BUSH, Douglas. "Milton." *The Renaissance and English Humanism.* Toronto: Univ. of Toronto Press, 1939, pp. 101–134. [Reprinted, 1941.]

510A CAMÉ, Jean-François. *Les structures fondamentales de l'univers imaginaire Miltonien.* Clamecy, France: Didier, 1976. [Études Anglaises 59]

511 CAREY, John. *Milton.* London: Evans, 1969. [An introductory survey of Milton's "more important poems."]

512 CHESTERTON, Gilbert K. "Milton: Man and Poet." *Catholic World,* 104 (1917), 463–470.

513 COLERIDGE, Samuel Taylor. *Coleridge on the Seventeenth Century.* Ed. Roberta F. Brinkley. Durham, N.C.: Duke Univ. Press, 1955 [Contains "Milton: Prose," pp. 471–473, and "Milton: Poetry," pp. 541–611.]

514 COLERIDGE, Samuel Taylor. "Milton." *The Literary Remains of Samuel Taylor Coleridge.* 4 vols. London: W. Pickering, 1836–1839.

515 CONDEE, Ralph Waterbury. *Structure in Milton's Poetry: From the Foundation to the Pinnacles.* University Park and London: Pennsylvania State Univ. Press, 1974.

516 CULLEN, Patrick. "John Milton." *The Infernal Triad: The Flesh, the World, and the Devil in Spenser and Milton.* Princeton: Princeton Univ. Press, 1974, pp. 97–250. [He discusses *PL, PR,* and *SA.*]

517 DAICHES, David. *Milton.* London and New York: Hutchinson's Universal Library, 1957. [Norton, 1966]†

518 DE QUINCEY, Thomas. "Life of Milton." *Blackwood's Magazine,* December, 1839.

519 DIEKHOFF, John S. "Critical Activity of the Poetic Mind: John Milton." *PMLA,* 55 (1940), 748–772.

520 DOWDEN, Edward. *Puritan and Anglican: Studies in Literature.* London: Kegan Paul, 1900. [2d edition. New York: Holt, 1901. Milton on liberty—civil, ecclesiastical and theological, pp. 133–197.]

521 EMERSON, Ralph Waldo. "Milton." *North American Review,* 47 (1838), 56–73.

521A FIXLER, Michael. *Milton and the Kingdoms of God.* Evanston: Northwestern Univ. Press; London: Faber & Faber, 1964, [See **1402.**]

522 FRENCH, J. Milton. "Milton and the Barbarous Dissonance." *TSLL,* 4 (1962), 376–389. [A survey of adverse criticism of Milton.]

523 FRYE, Northrop. *The Return of Eden: Five Essays on Milton's Epics.* Toronto: Univ. of Toronto Press, 1965. Reprinted as *Five Essays on Milton's Epics.* London: Routledge & Kegan Paul, 1966.

524 GRAVES, Robert. "The Ghost of Milton." *The Common Asphodel: Collected Essays on Poetry,* 1922–1949. London: Hamish Hamilton, 1949, pp. 315–325. [Milton as "a monster and a renegade."]

525 GRIERSON, Herbert J. C. *Cross Currents in English Literature of the* xvııth *Century; or, The World, the Flesh, & the Spirit, Their Actions & Reactions.* London: Chatto & Windus, 1929. [Torchbook, Penguin]† [Chapter VII is devoted to Milton.]

526 HANFORD, James Holly. *John Milton Poet and Humanist: Essays by James Holly Hanford.* Ed. John S. Diekhoff. Cleveland: The Press of Western Reserve Univ., 1966. [A reprint of eight previously published essays by Hanford: "The Youth of Milton," "The Chronology of Milton's Private Studies," "The Pastoral Elegy and Milton's *Lycidas,*" "Milton and the Return to Humanism," "Milton and the Art of War," "The Dramatic Element in *PL,*" "The Temptation Motive in Milton," and "*SA* and Milton in Old Age."]

527 HANFORD, James Holly, and TAAFE, James G. *A Milton Handbook.* 5th ed. New York: Appleton-Century-Crofts, 1970. [First published in 1926.]

528 HARDISON, O. B., Jr. "The Orator and the Poet: The Dilemma of Humanist Literature." *Journal of Medieval and Renaissance Studies,* 1 (1971), 33–44. [Reprinted in his *Toward Freedom and Dignity: The Humanities and the Idea of Humanity.* Baltimore: Johns Hopkins Press, 1972, pp. 61–83.]

528A HILL, Christopher, "Milton the Radical." *TLS,* 29 Nov 1974, pp. 1330–1332. [For responses in *TLS,* see **1151A.**]

528B HILL, Christopher. *Milton and the English Revolution.* New York: Viking, 1977.

529 HUGHES, Merritt Y. *Ten Perspectives on Milton.* New York and London: Yale Univ. Press, 1965.

530 HUTCHINSON, F. E. *Milton and the English Mind.* London: English Universities Press, 1950. [Collier, 1962]†

531 HYMAN, Lawrence W. *The Quarrel Within: Art and Morality in Milton's Poetry.* Port Washington, N.Y.: Kennikat, 1972.

532 KERRIGAN, William. "The Heretical Milton: From Assumption to Mortalism." *ELR,* 5 (1975), 125–166. [Finds a coherence between Milton's mortalist beliefs and evolving patterns in his poetry.]

533 KERRIGAN, William. *The Prophetic Milton.* Charlottesville: Univ. of Virginia Press, 1974. [Examines the major poems and pertinent minor poems and prose treatises in the context of prophetic inspiration.]

534 KNIGHT, G. Wilson. *Chariot of Wrath: the Message of John Milton to Democracy at War.* London: Faber & Faber, 1942. [Partially reprinted in *Poets of Action* (Methuen, 1967), pp. 70–162.]

535 KNIGHT, G. Wilson. "The Frozen Labyrinth: An Essay on Milton." *The Burning Oracle: Studies in the Poetry of Action.* London: Milford; Oxford: Oxford Univ. Press, 1939, pp. 59–113. [Reprinted in *Poets of Action* (Methuen, 1967), pp. 18–69.]

536 KRANIDAS, Thomas. "A View of Milton and the Traditional." *Milton Studies I* (1969), 15–29.

537 LAWRY, Jon S. *The Shadow of Heaven: Matter and Stance in Milton's Poetry.* Ithaca: Cornell Univ. Press, 1968.

538 LE COMTE, Edward. *Milton's Unchanging Mind: Three Essays.* Port Washington, N.Y. and London: Kennikat 1973. ["Milton versus Time," "Areopagitica as a Scenario for *Paradise Lost,*" and "The Satirist and Wit."]

539 LE COMTE, Edward S. *Yet Once More: Verbal and Psychological Pattern in Milton.* New York: Liberal Arts Press, 1953. [Reprinted by AMS, 1969.]

540 LEISHMAN, James B. "Some remarks on seventeenth-century poetry and Milton's place in it." *Milton's Minor Poems* (**746**) pp. 22–39.

GENERAL CRITICISM AND INTERPRETATION

541 LEWIS, C. S. "The Personal Heresy in Criticism" and "An Open Letter to Dr. Tillyard." E&S, 19 (1934), 7–28, and 21 (1936), 153–168. [Parts of a discussion with E. M. W. Tillyard.]

542 LOWELL, James Russell. "Milton." *Among My Books. Second Series.* Boston: Houghton, Mifflin, 1876.

543 MACAULAY, Thomas B. "Milton." *Edinburgh Review,* 84 (1825), 304–346.

544 MAHOOD, M. M. "Milton's Heroes." *Poetry and Humanism.* New Haven: Yale Univ. Press; London: Jonathan Cape, 1950, pp. 207–251. [Norton, 1970]† [Reprinted in **496.**]

545 MARILLA, E. L. *Milton and Modern Man: Selected Essays.* University, Alabama: Univ. of Alabama Press, 1968.

546 MARSHALL, Margaret Wiley. "Milton and Heresy: Guidelines for a Sketch." *Critical Essays on English Literature Presented to Professor M.ʾS. Duraiswami.* Ed. Dr. V. S. Seturaman. Bombay, Calcutta, Madras, New Delhi: Orient Longmans, 1965, pp. 40–56. [The subject is not actually heresy, but ways of knowing.]

547 MARTZ, Louis L. "The Rising Poet, 1645." *The Lyric and Dramatic Milton: Selected Papers from the English Institute.* Ed. Joseph H. Summers **(498)** pp. 3–33. [Partially reprinted in **497.**]

548 MINER, Earl. "Milton's Laws Divine and Human." *The Restoration Mode from Milton to Dryden.* Princeton: Princeton Univ. Press, 1974, pp. 198–287.

549 NICOLSON, Marjorie Hope. *John Milton: A Reader's Guide to His Poetry.* New York: Farrar, Straus, 1963. [Noonday]†

550 PECK, Francis. *New Memoirs of the Life and Poetical Works of Mr. John Milton: With I. An Examination of Milton's Stile: And, II. Explanatory & Critical Notes on Divers Passages of Milton & Shakespeare* [and other topics, including addition of spurious works to Milton canon]. London, 1740.

551 POTTER, Lois. *A Preface to Milton.* London: Longman, 1971; New York: Scribner's. 1972.

552 RAJAN, Balachandra. *The Lofty Rhyme: A Study of Milton's Major Poetry.* Coral Gables: Univ. of Miami Press, 1970. [Chs. on Nativity Ode, *Comus, Lycidas, PL, PR,* and *SA.*]

553 RAJAN, Balachandra. " 'To Which is Added *Samson Agonistes—*'." *The Prison and the Pinnacle,* ed. B. Rajan **(495),** pp. 82–110. [The relationship of *PR* and *SA,* and their place in Milton's work.]

554 RALEIGH, Sir Walter A. *Milton.* London: E. Arnold; New York: Putnam, 1900. [Parts of Chs. V and VI reprinted in **499.**]

554A RICHMOND, Hugh M. *The Christian Revolutionary: John Milton.* Berkeley, Los Angeles, London: Univ. of California Press, 1974.

555 RIVERS, Isabel. "John Milton: Reformation and Regeneration." *The Poetry of Conservatism 1600–1745: A Study of Poets and Public Affairs from Jonson to Pope.* Cambridge: Rivers Press, 1973, pp. 74–100. [Milton's evolving thought concerning the poet's role and the individual in society.]

556 ROSS, Malcolm M. *Milton's Royalism: A Study of the Conflict of Symbol and Idea in the Poems.* Ithaca: Cornell Univ. Press, 1943.

557 SAMPSON, Alden. *Studies in Milton and an Essay on Poetry.* New York: Moffat, Yard, 1913. [Chapters: "From *Lycidas to Paradise Lost.*" "Milton's Confession of Faith." "Certain Aspects of the Poetic Genius." Appendix I: "The Bust of Milton." Appendix II: "Sir Henry Vane and Harvard College."]

557A SAMUEL, Irene. "The Development of Milton's Poetics." *PMLA,* 92 (1977), 231–240.

558 SAURAT, Denis. *Milton et le matérialisme chrétien en Angleterre.* Paris: Rieder, 1928.

559 SAURAT, Denis. *Milton: Man and Thinker.* London: Jonathan Cape; New York: Dial Press, 1925. [2d edition, London: Dent, 1944; reprinted, 1946.]

560 SAURAT, Denis. *La pensée de Milton.* Paris: Alcan, 1920.

561 SHAWCROSS, John T., ed. *Milton: The Critical Heritage.* New York: Barnes & Noble, 1970. [Selected commentary on Milton and his work from 1628 to 1731.]

562 SHAWCROSS, John T., ed. *Milton 1732–1801: The Critical Heritage.* London and Boston: Routledge & Kegan Paul, 1972. [Selected commentary on Milton and his work from 1732 to 1801.]

563 STEADMAN, John M. *Milton and the Renaissance Hero.* Oxford: Clarendon Press, 1967. [A study of the major poetry in the light of Renaissance theories of heroism, stressing Milton's innovations on the epic tradition.]

564 STEADMAN, John M. *Milton's Epic Characters: Image and Idol.* Chapel Hill: Univ. of North Carolina Press, 1968. [The major poems are examined in relation to their intellectual backgrounds, with particular emphasis on problems of characterization.]

565 SUMMERS, Joseph H. "Milton and the Cult of Conformity." *Yale Review,* 46 (1957), 511–527. [Reprinted in **496.**]

566 TAINE, H. "Milton: Son génie et ses œuvres." *Revue des deux mondes,* 9 (1857), 818–854.

567. THOMPSON, Elbert N. S. *Essays on Milton.* New Haven. Yale Univ. Press, 1914. [Chapters: "Milton, the Last of the Elizabethans." "Milton's Temperament and Ideals." "The True Bearing of Milton's Prose." "The Epic Structure of *Paradise Lost.*" "The Sources of *Paradise Lost.*" "The Theme of *Paradise Lost.*" "Milton's Art."]

568 TILLYARD, E. M. W. *The Miltonic Setting: Past and Present.* Cambridge: Cambridge Univ. Press; New York: Macmillan, 1938. [Reprinted, 1947.] [Chapters: " 'L'Allegro' and 'Il Penseroso'." "Milton and Keats." "Milton and Primitive Feeling." "Milton and Prophetic Poetry." "Milton and Protestantism." "Milton's Visual Imagination." "Milton's Style." "Milton and the English Epic Tradition." "The Growth of Milton's Epic Plans."] [Reprinted by Barnes and Noble, 1966.]

569 TILLYARD, E. M. W. *Studies in Milton.* London: Chatto & Windus; New York: Macmillan, 1951. [Chapters: "Arnold on Milton." "The Crisis of *Paradise Lost.*" "A Note on Satan." "Satan, Gabriel and the Plowman." "Adam and Eve in Paradise." "Milton's Humour." "The Action of *Comus.*" "The Christ of *Paradise Regained.*" "Private Correspondence and Academic Exercises." "Theology and Emotion in Milton." "Milton and Statius." "Milton and Philostratus." [Ch. 2, "The Crisis of *Paradise Lost,*" is reprinted in **489.**]

37

570 TUVE, Rosemond. *Essays by Rosemond Tuve.* Ed. Thomas P. Roche, Jr. Princeton: Princeton Univ. Press, 1970. [Contains two essays on Milton: "New Approaches to Milton," pp. 255–261, and "Baroque and Mannerist Milton?" pp. 262–280.]

570A TUVE, Rosemond. *Images and Themes in Five Poems by Milton.* Cambridge: Harvard Univ. Press, 1957. [The five poems are: "On the Morning of Christ's Nativity," "L'allegro," "Il Penseroso," *Comus,* and "Lycedas."]

571 VISIAK, E. H. *The Portent of Milton: Some Aspects of His Genius.* London: W. Laurie, 1958.

572 VOLTAIRE, François. *Essay on Milton.* Ed. Desmond Flower. Cambridge: Cambridge Univ. Press, 1954.

573 WATKINS, W. B. C. *An Anatomy of Milton's Verse.* Baton Rouge: Louisiana State Univ. Press, 1955; Hamden, Conn.: Archon, 1965. [Ch. 2, "Creation," is reprinted in **489**.]

574 WILLIAMS, Charles. "Milton." *The English Poetic Mind.* Oxford: Clarendon Press, 1932, pp. 110–152. [Reprinted: New York: Russell & Russell, 1963; also reprinted in Williams' *Selected Writings,* ed. Anne Ridler, 1961.]

575 WILLIAMSON, George. *Milton and Others.* Chicago: Univ. of Chicago Press; London: Faber & Faber, 1965. [Contains the following essays on Milton: "Milton the Anti-Romantic," "The Context of *Comus.*" "The Education of Adam," "Plot in *Paradise Regained,*" "Tension in *Samson Agonistes,*" "Dryden's View of Milton."]

576 WOODBERRY, George Edward. *Great Writers: Cervantes, Scott, Milton, Virgil, Montaigne, Shakespeare.* New York: Macmillan, 1912.

577 WOODHOUSE, A. S. P. *The Heavenly Muse: A Preface to Milton.* Ed. Hugh MacCallum. Toronto: Univ. of Toronto Press, 1972. [A reprint of Woodhouse's published essays on Milton, with previously unpublished materials edited by MacCallum.]

Studies of Individual Works

Latin Poetry

578 ALLEN, Don Cameron. "John Milton, Elegy Five: 'In Adventum Veris'." *Image and Meaning: Metaphoric Traditions in Renaissance Poetry.* Baltimore: Johns Hopkins Press, 1968. pp. 115–137.

579 ALLEN, Don Cameron. "Milton as a Latin Poet." *Neo-Latin Poetry of the Sixteenth and Seventeenth Centuries: Papers ... Presented at a Seminar Held on October 17, 1967 at the Clark Library.* Los Angeles: Clark Library, 1965. pp. 30–52. Reprinted in *Stuart and Georgian Moments.* Ed. Earl Miner. Berkeley: Univ. of California Press, 1971. pp. 23–45.

580 BRADNER, Leicester. "Milton." *Musae Anglicanae: A History of Anglo-Latin Poetry 1500–1925.* New York: Modern Language Association; London: Oxford Univ. Press, 1940. pp. 111–118.

581 BUSH, Douglas. "The Date of Milton's *Ad Pątrem.*" *MP,* 61 (1964), 204–208. [Argues for 1631–1632 instead of the traditional 1634 or 1637.]

582 BUSH, Douglas. "Introduction." Vol. I of *A Variorum Commentary on the Poems of John Milton* (16), pp. 3–24.

583 CAREY, John. "Milton's *Ad Patrem,* 35–37." *RES,* 15 (1964), 180–184. [The " *spiritus* . . . *igneus*" with its *"inenarrabile carmen"* is Milton's own spirit.]

584 CONDEE, Ralph W. "The Latin Poetry of John Milton." *The Latin Poetry of English Poets.* Ed. J. W. Binns. London and Boston: Routledge & Kegan Paul, 1974. pp. 58–92.

585 CONDEE, Ralph W. *Structure in Milton's Poetry: From the Foundations to the Pinnacles.* University Park and London: Pennsylvania State Univ. Press, 1974. [Discusses Elegies I, III, V, "In Obitum Procancellari Medici," "Ad Patrem," "Mansus," and "Epitaphium Damonis."]

586 DE FILIPPIS, Michele. "Milton and Manso: Cups or Books?" *PMLA,* 51(1936), 745–756.

587 HANFORD, James Holly. "The Youth of Milton: An Interpretation of His Early Literary Development." *Studies in Shakespeare, Milton, and Donne.* New York: Macmillan, 1925. pp. 89–163. [Reprinted in **526**]

588 MACKELLAR, Walter, ed. *The Latin Poems of John Milton.* New Haven: Yale Univ. Press for Cornell Univ.; London: Milford, 1930. Reprinted by Somerset Publishers.

589 NICOLS, Fred J. " 'Lycidas,' 'Epitaphium Damonis,' the Empty Dream, and the Failed Song." *Acta Conventus Neo-Latini Lovaniensis: Proceedings of the First International Congress of Neo-Latin Studies,* Louvain, 23–28 August 1971. Ed. J. Ijsewijn and Eckhard Kessler. Munich: Wilhelm Fink; Louvain: Louvain Univ. Press, 1973. pp. 445–452.

590 PARKER, William Riley. "Notes on the Chronology of Milton's Latin Poems." *A Tribute to George Coffin Taylor: Studies and Essays, Chiefly Elizabethan, by His Students and Friends.* Ed. Arnold Williams. Chapel Hill: Univ. of North Carolina Press, 1952. pp. 113–131.

591 RAND, E. K. "Milton in Rustication." *SP,* 19 (1922), 109–135. [Milton's study of ancient poets and their influence on him.]

592 SEMPLE, W. H. "The Latin Poems of John Milton." *BJRL,* 46 (1963), 217–235. [Sympathetic commentary by a Latinist, mainly on the autobiographical poems.]

Nativity Ode

593 ALLEN, Don Cameron. "The Higher Compromise: *On the Morning of Christ's Nativity* and *A Mask.*" *The Harmonious Vision* (**501**), pp. 24–40.

594 BARKER, Arthur E. "The Pattern of Milton's Nativity Ode." *UTQ,* 10 (1941), 167–181. [Reprinted in **496**.]

594A BEHRENDT, Stephen. "Blake's Illustrations to Milton's Nativity Ode." *PQ,* 55 (1976), 65–95.

595 BROADBENT, John B. "The Nativity Ode." *The Living Milton.* Ed. Frank Kermode (**486**), pp. 12–31.

595A CHAMBERS, A. B. "Christmas: The Liturgy of the Church and English Verse of the Renaissance." *Literary Monographs,* vol. 6. Ed. Eric Rothstein and J. A. Wittreich, Jr. Madison: Univ. of Wisconsin Press, 1975, pp. 109–153.

596 COOK, Albert S. "Notes on Milton's 'On the Morning of Christ's Nativity'." *Transactions of the Connecticut Academy of Arts and Sciences,* 15 (1909), 307–368.

596A DAVIES, H. Neville. "Laid Artfully Together: Stanzaic Design in Milton's 'On the Morning of Christ's Nativity'." *Fair Forms.* Ed. Maren-Sofie Røstvig. Cambridge, England: D. S. Brewer, 1975, pp. 85–117.

597 KASTOR, Frank S. "Milton's Narrative: 'Christ's Nativity'." *Anglia,* 86 (1968), 339–352.

598 KINGSLEY, Lawrence W. "Mythic Dialectic in the Nativity Ode." *Milton Studies IV* (1972), 163–176.

599 MCQUEEN, William A. "Redeeming Time: Milton's 'On the Morning of Christ's Nativity'." *Renaissance Papers 1975,* pp. 53–61.

600 MORRIS, David B. "Drama and Stasis in Milton's 'Ode on the Morning of Christ's Nativity'." *SP,* 68 (1971), 207–222.

601 NELSON, Lowry, Jr. "Milton's 'Nativity Ode'." *Baroque Lyric Poetry.* New Haven and London: Yale Univ. Press, 1961. pp. 41–51.

602 PATRIDES, C. A. " 'The Cessation of the Oracles': The History of a Legend." *MLR,* 60 (1965), 500–507.

602A PECHEUX, Mother Mary Christopher. "The Image of The Sun in Milton's 'Nativity Ode'." *HLQ,* 38, (1975), 315–333.

603 RAJAN, Balachandra. "In Order Serviceable." *MLR,* 63 (1968), 13–22. [Reprinted in **552**].

603A ROLLINSON, Philip. "Milton's Nativity Poem and the Decorum of Genre." *Milton Studies VII* (1975), 165–188.

603B RØSTVIG, Maren-Sofie. " 'Elaborate Song': Conceptual Structure in Milton's 'On the Morning of Christ's Nativity.' " *Fair Forms.* Ed. Maren-Sofie Røstvig. Cambridge, Eng: D. S. Brewer, 1975. pp. 54–72 [See **1612, 1639.**]

604 SWAIM, Kathleen M. " 'Mighty Pan': Tradition and an Image in Milton's Nativity *Hymn.*" *SP,* 68 (1971), 484–495.

605 TUVE, Rosemond. "The Hymn on the Morning of Christ's Nativity." *Images and Themes in Five Poems by Milton.* Cambridge, Mass.: Harvard Univ. Press, 1957. pp. 37–72.

L'Allegro and Il Penseroso

606 ALLEN, Don Cameron. "The Search for the Prophetic Strain: 'L'Allegro' and 'Il Penseroso'." *The Harmonious Vision* (**501**), pp. 3–23.

607 BABB, Lawrence. "The Background of 'Il Penseroso'." *SP,* 37 (1940), 257–273.

607A BEHRENDT, Stephen. "Bright Pilgrimage: William Blakes Designs for *L'Allegro* and *Il Penseroso.*" *Milton Studies VIII* (1975), 123–147.

608 BROOKS, Cleanth. "The Light Symbolism in 'L'Allegro' and 'Il Penseroso'." *The Well Wrought Urn: Studies in the Structure of Poetry.* New York: Reynal & Hitchcock, 1947; London: Dobson, 1949. pp. 47–61. [Harvest]†

609 CARPENTER, Nan Cooke. "The Place of Music in *L'Allegro* and *Il Penseroso.* " *UTQ,* 22 (1953), 354–367.

609A COUNCIL, Norman B. "*L'Allegro, Il Pensaroso,* and 'the Cycle of Universal Knowledge." *Milton Studies IX* (1976), 203–219.

610 DEMPSEY, Ivey. "To 'Attain to Something Like Prophetic Strain'." *Papers on Milton.* Ed. Philip M. Griffith and Lester F. Zimmerman **(484)**, pp. 9–24.

610A FISH, Stanley E. "What It's Like to Read *L'Allegro* and *Il Penseroso.* " *Milton Studies VII* (1975), 77–99.

611 GECKLE, George L. "Miltonic Idealism: *L'Allegro* and *Il Penseroso.* " *TSLL,* 9 (1968), 455–473.

612 HARTMAN, Geoffrey. "False Themes and Gentle Minds." *PQ,* 47 (1968), 55–68. [Although his focus is on later authors, Hartman devotes five pages to *L'Allegro-Il Penseroso* series viewed as "a romantic struggle with Romance." The article is reprinted in *Beyond Formalism* (Yale, 1970).]

613 LEISHMAN, J. B. "*L'Allegro* and *Il Penseroso* in Their Relationship to Seventeenth-Century Poetry." *E & S* 4 (1951), 1–36. [Reprinted in **746** and in **496**.]

613A LYONS, Bridget Gellert. *Voices of Melancholy,* New York: Barnes and Noble, 1971, pp. 151–156.†

614 MILLER, David M. "From Delusion to Illumination: A Larger Structure for 'L'Allegro'-'Il Penseroso'." *PMLA,* 86 (1971), 32–39.

614A PATTERSON, Annabel. "*L'Allegro, Il Penseroso,* and *Comus:* The Logic of Recombination." *Milton Q,* 9 (1975), 75–79.

615 STRINGER, Gary. "The Unity of 'L'Allegro' and 'Il Penseroso'." *TSLL,* 12 (1970), 221–229.

615A SWAIM, Kathleen M. "Cycle and Circle: Time and Structure in *L'Allegro* and *Il Penseroso.* " *TSLL,* 18 (1976), 422–432.

616 TATE, Eleanor. "Milton's 'L'Allegro' and 'Il Penseroso'—Balance, Progression, or Dichotomy?" *MLN,* 76 (1961), 585–590.

617 TILLYARD, E. M. W. *Milton: L'Allegro and Il Penseroso* (English Association Pamphlet 82). Oxford: Oxford Univ. Press, 1932. [Reprinted in **568.**]

618 TUVE, Rosemond. "The Structural Figures of *L'Allegro* and *Il Penseroso.* " *Images and Themes in Five Poems by Milton* **(570A)**, pp. 15–36. [Reprinted in **476.**]

619 VIA, John A. "The Rhythm of Regenerate Experience: *L'Allegro* and *Il Penseroso.* " *Renaissance Papers 1969,* pp. 47–55.

Sonnets

620 BUDICK, Sanford. "On the Late Massacre in Piemont." *Poetry of Civilization* **(507)**, pp. 42–45.

621 CONDEE, Ralph W. "Milton's Gaudy-Day with Lawrence." *Directions in Literary Criticism: Contemporary Approaches to Literature.* Ed. Stanley Weintraub and Philip Young, University Park: Pennsylvania State Univ. Press, 1973, pp. 86–92.

622 DAHLBERG, Charles R. "Milton's Sonnet 23 on His 'Late Espoused Saint'." *N&Q,* 194 (1949), 321.

STUDIES OF INDIVIDUAL WORKS

623 FINLEY, John H., Jr. "Milton and Horace: A Study of Milton's Sonnets." *Harvard Studies in Classical Philology,* 48 (1937), 29–73.

624 FISKE, Dixon. "Milton in the Middle of Life: Sonnet XIX." *ELH,* 41 (1974), 37–49.

624A FISKE, Dixon. "The Theme of Purification in Milton's Sonnet XXIII." *Milton Studies VIII* (1975), 149–163.

625 GOSSMAN, Ann, and WHITING, George W. "Milton's First Sonnet on His Blindness." *RES,* 12 (1961), 364–370.

626 HANFORD, James Holly. "The Arrangement and Dates of Milton's Sonnets." *MP,* 18 (1921), 475–483.

627 HONIGMANN, E. A. J. *Milton's Sonnets.* London: Macmillan; New York: St. Martins, 1966.

628 KELLEY, Maurice. "Milton's Later Sonnets and the Cambridge Manuscript." *MP,* 54 (1956), 20–25.

629 LE COMTE, Edward S. "The Veiled Face of Milton's Wife." *N&Q,* N.S. 1 (1954), 245–246.

629A LOW, Anthony. "Milton's Last Sonnet." *Milton Q,* 9 (1975), 80–82.

629B MCCARTHY, William. "The Continuity of Milton's Sonnets." *PMLA,* 92 (1977), 96–109.

630 MORSE, C. J. "The Dating of Milton's Sonnet XIX." *TLS,* 15 Sept., 1961, p. 620.

631 PARKER, William R. "The Dates of Milton's Sonnets on Blindness." *PMLA,* 73 (1958), 196–200.

632 PARKER, William R. "Milton's Last Sonnet: Addressed to First or Second Wife?" *RES,* 21 (1945), 235–238.

633 PARKER, William R. "Milton's Last Sonnet Again." *RES,* N.S. 2 (1951), 147–152.

634 PRINCE, F. T. "Milton's Sonnets." *The Italian Element in Milton's Verse,* Oxford: Clarendon Press, 1962, pp. 89–107.

635 PYLE, Fitzroy. "Milton's First Sonnet on His Blindness." *RES,* 9 (1958), 376–387.

636 PYLE, Fitzroy. "Milton's Sonnet on His 'Late Espoused Saint.' " *RES,* 25 (1949), 57–60.

637 ROBINS, Harry F. "Milton's First Sonnet on His Blindness." *RES,* N.S. 7 (1956), 360–366.

638 SHAWCROSS, John T. "Of Chronology and the Dates of Milton's Translation from Horace and the *New Forcers of Conscience.* " *SEL,* 3 (1963), 77–84.

639 SLAKEY, Roger L. "Milton's Sonnet 'On His Blindness'." *ELH,* 28 (1960), 122–130.

640 SMART, John S. *The Sonnets of Milton.* Glasgow: Maclehose, Jackson, 1921. Reprinted by Clarendon Press, 1966.†

641 STEVENS, David H. "The Order of Milton's Sonnets." *MP,* 17 (1919), 25–33.

642 STOEHR, Taylor. "Syntax and Poetic Form in Milton's Sonnets." *ES,* 45 (1964), 289–301. [The technique of the sonnets discussed in terms derived from structural linguistics.]

643 STROUP, Thomas B. "Aeneas' Vision of Creusa and Milton's Twenty-third Sonnet." *PQ,* 39 (1960), 125–126.

644 STROUP, Thomas B. " 'When I Consider': Milton's Sonnet XIX." *SP,* 69 (1972), 242–258.

645 SVENDSEN, Kester. "Milton's Sonnet on the Massacre in Piedmont." *Shakespeare Association Bulletin,* 20 (1945), 147–155.

646 WHEELER, Thomas. "Milton's Twenty-third Sonnet." *SP,* 58 (1961), 510–515.

647 WILLIAMSON, Marilyn L. "A Reading of Milton's Twenty-third Sonnet." *Milton Studies IV* (1972), 141–149.

Comus

648 ADAMS, Robert M. "Reading *Comus.*" *MP,* 51 (1953), 18–32.

649 ALLEN, Don Cameron. "The Higher Compromise: *On The Morning of Christ's Nativity* and *A Mask.*" *The Harmonious Vision* (**501**), pp. 24–40.

650 ALLEN, Don C. "Milton's *Comus* as a Failure in Artistic Compromise." *ELH,* 16 (1949), 104–119.

651 ARTHOS, John. On *"A Mask Presented at Ludlow-Castle."* Ann Arbor: Univ. of Michigan Press, 1954.

652 ARTHOS, John. "The Realms of Being in the Epilogue of *Comus.*" *MLN,* 76 (1961), 321–324.

652A BAKER, Stewart A. "Eros and the Three Shepherds of *Comus.*" *Rice University Studies,* 61 (1975), 13–26.

653 BARBER, C. L. "A Mask Presented at Ludlow Castle: The Masque as a Masque." *The Lyric and Dramatic Milton: Selected Papers from the English Institute.* Ed. Joseph H. Summers (**498**), pp. 35–63.

654 BERCOVITCH, Sacvan. "Milton's 'Haemony': Knowledge and Belief." *HLQ,* 33 (1970), 351–359. [Cf. **681**.]

655 BOYETTE, Purvis E. "Milton's Abstracted Sublimities: The Structure of Meaning in *A Mask.*" *TSE,* 18 (1970), 35–58.

656 BREASTED, Barbara. "*Comus* and the Castelhaven Scandal." *Milton Studies III* (1971), 201–224.

657 BRIE, F. "Das Märchen von Childe Rowland und sein Nachleben." *Palaestra,* 148 (1925), 118–143. [Relationship to *Comus.*]

658 DEMARAY, John G. *Milton and the Masque Tradition: The Early Poems,* "Arcades" *and Comus.* Cambridge: Harvard Univ. Press, 1968.

659 DIEKHOFF, John S., ed. *A Masque at Ludlow: Essays on Milton's Comus.* Cleveland: The Press of Case Western Reserve Univ., 1968. [A collection of ten previously published essays with the text of the Bridgewater version of *Comus,* Henry Lawes' songs, and an essay on "The Text of *Comus,* 1634 to 1645."]

660 DYSON, A. E. "The Interpretation of *Comus.*" *E&S,* N.S. 8 (1955), 89–114.

661 FINNEY, Gretchen Ludke. "*Comus, Drama per Musica.*" *SP,* 37 (1940), 482–500.

STUDIES OF INDIVIDUAL WORKS

661A FISH, Stanley E. "Problem Solving in *Comus.*" *Illustrious Evidence.* Ed. Earl Miner. Berkeley and Los Angeles: Univ. of California Press, 1975. pp. 115–131.

662 FLETCHER, Angus. *The Transcendental Masque: An Essay on Milton's Comus.* Ithaca and London: Cornell Univ. Press, 1971.

663 HAUN, Eugene. "An Inquiry into the Genre of *Comus.*" *Essays in Honor of Walter Clyde Curry.* Nashville, Tenn.: Vanderbilt Univ. Press, 1954. pp. 221–239.

663A HIEATT, A. Kent. *"Fairie Queene* II, III and *Comus.*" *Chaucer, Shakespeare, Milton.* Montreal and London: McGill-Queen's Univ. Press, 1975. pp. 153–168.

664 JAYNE, Sears. "The Subject of Milton's Ludlow *Mask.*" *PMLA,* 74 (1959), 533–543. [Reprinted in **476.**]

665 KLEIN, Joan Larsen. "Some Spenserian Influences on Milton's *Comus.*" *AnM,* 5 (1964), 27–47.

666 KOHN, Terry Kidner. "Landscape in the Transcendent Masque." *Milton Studies VI* (1975), 143–164.

667 LA GUARDIA, Eric. "Milton's Comus." *Nature Redeemed: The Imitation of Order in Three Renaissance Poems.* The Hague: Mouton, 1966. pp. 126–147.

668 LE COMTE, Edward. "New Light on the Haemony Passage in *Comus.*" *PQ,* 21 (1942), 283–298.

669 MAJOR, John M. *"Comus* and *The Tempest.*" *SQ,* 10 (1959), 177–183.

669A MARTZ, Louis L. "The Music of Comus." *Illustrious Evidence.* Ed. Earl Miner. Berkeley and Los Angeles: Univ. of California Press, 1975. pp. 93–113.

670 MAXWELL, J. C. "The Pseudo-Problem of *Comus.*" *Cambridge Journal,* 1 (1948), 376–380. [The doctrine of virtue.]

671 NEUSE, Richard. "Metamorphosis and Symbolic Action in *Comus.*" *ELH,* 34 (1967), 49–64. [Reprinted in **479.**]

672 ORUCH, Jack B. "Imitation and Invention in the Sabrina Myths of Drayton and Milton." *Anglia,* 90 (1972), 60–70.

673 OTTEN, Charlotte F. "Milton's Haemony." *ELR,* 5 (1975), 81–95. ["An attempt to identify 'haemony' by consulting herbals, health manuals, magico-medical books, and theological treatises."]

673A PATTERSON, Annabel. *"L'Allegro, Il Penseroso,* and *Comus:* The Logic of Recombination." *Milton Q,* 9 (1975), 75–79.

674 RAJAN, Balachandra. *"Comus:* The Inglorious Likeness." *UTQ,* 37 (1968), 113–135. [Reprinted in **552.**]

675 ROSENBERG, D. M. "Milton's Masque: A Social Occasion for Philosophic Laughter." *SP,* 67 (1970), 245–253.

676 SAVAGE, J. B. *"Comus* and Its Tradition." *ELR,* 5 (1975), 58–80. [Interprets *Comus* as a Platonic, rather than a Christian, masque.]

677 SCOFUS, Alice-Lyle. "The Mysteries in Milton's Masque." *Milton Studies VI* (1975), 113–142.

678 SENSABAUGH, George F. "The *Milieu* of *Comus.*" *SP,* 41 (1944), 238–249.

679 SHAWCROSS, John T. "Henry Lawes's Settings of Songs for Milton's *Comus.* " *JRUL,* 28 (1964), 22–28. [Examination of mss shows the uncertainty of modern conclusions about the original form of the work.]

680 SPROTT, S. E., ed. *John Milton: A Maske: The Earlier Versions.* Toronto and Buffalo: Univ. of Toronto Press, 1973.

681 STEADMAN, John M. "Milton's Haemony: Etymology and Allegory." *PMLA,* 77 (1962), 200–207. [Cf. **654**.]

682 SWAIM, Kathleen M. "An Ovidian Analogue for *Comus.*" *Milton Quarterly,* 9 (1975), 14–17.

683 TILLYARD, E. M. W. "The Action of *Comus.*" *Studies in Milton* (**569**), pp. 82–99.

684 TUVE, Rosemond. "Image, Form and Theme in *A Mask.*" *Images and Themes in Five Poems by Milton* (**570A**), pp. 112–161.

685 WELSFORD, Enid. *The Court Masque.* Cambridge: Cambridge Univ. Press, 1927. [Important background for *Arcades* and *Comus.*]

686 WILKENFELD, Roger B. "A Seat at the Center: An Interpretation of *Comus.*" *ELH,* 33 (1966), 170–197. [Reprinted in **479**.]

687 WILKINSON, David. "The Escape from Pollution: A Comment on *Comus.*" *EIC,* 10 (1960), 32–43.

688 WILLIAMSON, George. "The Context of *Comus.*" *Milton and Others* (**575**), pp. 26–41.

689 WOODHOUSE, A. S. P. "The Argument of Milton's *Comus.*" *UTQ,* 11 (1941), 46–71. [Reprinted in **577**.]

690 WOODHOUSE, A. S. P. "*Comus* Once More." *UTQ,* 19 (1950), 218–223. [Reprinted in **577**.]

Lycidas

691 ABRAMS, M. H. "Five Ways of Reading *Lycidas.*" *Varieties of Literary Experience: Eighteen Essays in World Literature,* Ed. Stanley Burnshaw. New York: New York Univ. Press, 1962, pp. 1–29. [First appeared in **723** under the title "Five Types of *Lycidas.*"]

692 ADAMS, Richard P. "The Archetypal Pattern of Death and Rebirth in Milton's *Lycidas.*" *PMLA,* 64 (1949), 183–188. [Reprinted in slightly condensed form in **493**.]

693 ADAMS, Robert M. "Bounding *Lycidas.*" *Hudson Review,* 23 (1970), 293–304.

694 ALLEN, Don Cameron. "The Translation of the Myth: The Epicedia and *Lycidas.*" *The Harmonious Vision* (**501**), pp. 41–70.

695 AUSTIN, Warren B. "Milton's *Lycidas* and Two Latin Elegies by Giles Fletcher, the Elder." *SP,* 44 (1947), 41–55.

696 BAKER, Stewart A. "Milton's Uncouth Swain." *Milton Studies III* (1971), 35–53.

697 BATTESTIN, Martin C. "John Crowe Ransom and *Lycidas:* A Reappraisal." *CE,* 17 (1955–1956), 223–228. [A rebuttal of **726**.]

698 BRETT, R. L. "Milton's *Lycidas.*" *Reason and Imagination: A Study of Form and Meaning in Four Poems.* London, New York, Toronto: Oxford Univ. Press for the Univ. of Hull, 1960, pp. 21–50.

STUDIES OF INDIVIDUAL WORKS

699 COFFMAN, George R. "The Parable of the Good Shepherd, *De Contemptu Mundi,* and *Lycidas:* Excerpts from a Chapter on Literary History and Culture." *ELH,* 3 (1936), 101–113.

700 COOLIDGE, John S. "Boethius and 'That Last Infirmity of Noble Mind.' " *PQ,* 42 (1963), 176–182.

701 DAICHES, David. *A Study of Literature for Readers and Critics.* Ithaca: Cornell Univ. Press, 1948. [Pp. 170–195 discuss *Lycidas.* Reprinted in **493** and **517**.]

702 ELLEDGE, Scott. *Milton's "Lycidas" Edited to Serve as an Introduction to Criticism.* New York: Harper and Row, 1966.

703 FELSEN, Karl E. "The 'Two-Handed Engine': A Balanced View." *Milton Quarterly,* 9 (1975), 6–14.

704 FINNEY, Gretchen Ludke. "A Musical Background for 'Lycidas.' " *HLQ,* 15 (1952), 325–350.

705 FLETCHER, Harris F. "Milton's 'Old Damoetas'." *JEGP,* 60 (1961), 250–257.

706 FORREST, James F. "The Significance of Milton's 'Mantle-Blue'." *Milton Quarterly,* 8 (1974), 41–48.

707 FRIEDMAN, Donald M. "*Lycidas:* The Swain's Paideia." *Milton Studies III* (1971), 3–34.

708 FRYE, Northrop. "Literature as Context: Milton's 'Lycidas'." *Comparative Literature: Proceedings of the Second Congress of the International Comparative Literature Association.* Ed. Werner P. Friederich. 2 vols. Chapel Hill: Univ. of North Carolina Press, 1959, vol. I, 44–45. [Reprinted in **493**.]

709 HANFORD, James Holly. "The Pastoral Elegy and Milton's 'Lycidas'." *PMLA,* 25 (1910), 403–447. [Reprinted in **493** and **526**.]

710 HARRISON, Thomas Perrin, Jr. *The Pastoral Elegy: An Anthology.* With translations by Harry Joshua Leon. Austin: Univ. of Texas Press, 1939.

711 HOWARD, Leon. " 'That Two-Handed Engine' Once More." *HLQ,* 15 (1952), 173–184.

711A LAMBERT, Ellen Zetzel. " 'Lycidas': Finding the Time and the Place." *Placing Sorrow.* Chapel Hill: Univ. of North Carolina Press, 1976, pp. 154–186.

712 LAWRY, Jon S. " 'Eager Thought': Dialectic in 'Lycidas.' " *PMLA,* 77 (1962), 27–32.

713 LE COMTE, Edward S. " 'Lycidas,' Petrarch, and the Plague." *MLN,* 69 (1954), 402–404.

714 LE COMTE, Edward S. " 'That Two-Handed Engine' and Savonarola." *SP,* 47 (1950), 589–606.

715 LE COMTE, Edward S. " 'That Two-Handed Engine' and Savonarola: Supplement." *SP,* 49 (1952), 548–550.

716 MACCAFFREY, Isabel G. "Lycidas: The Poet in a Landscape." *The Lyric and Dramatic Milton: Selected Papers from the English Institute.* Ed. Joseph H. Summers (498), pp. 65–92.

717 MARTZ, Louis L. "Who is Lycidas?" *Yale French Studies,* 47 (1972), 170–188.

718 MAYERSON, Caroline W. "The Orpheus Image in *Lycidas.*" *PMLA,* 64 (1949), 189–207.

46

719 MILES, Josephine. "Words as Themes in Milton's *Lycidas.*" *Poetry and Change.* Berkeley, Los Angeles, London: Univ. of California Press, 1974, pp. 84–90.

720 MUSTARD, Wilfred P. "Later Echoes of the Greek Bucolic Poets." *AJP,* 30 (1909), 245–283.

721 NASSAR, Eugene Paul. "Lycidas as Pastiche." *The Rape of Cinderella: Essays in Literary Continuity.* Bloomington and London: Indiana Univ. Press, 1970, pp. 16–27.

722 NELSON, Lowry, Jr. "Milton's 'Lycidas'." *Baroque Lyric Poetry* (601), pp. 64–76. Also pp. 138–152.

723 PATRIDES, C. A., ed. *Milton's Lycidas: The Tradition and the Poem.* New York: Holt, Rinehart, and Winston, 1961. [For a description of the contents, see **493**.]

723A PECHEUX, Mother Mary Christopher. "The Dread Voice in *Lycidas.*" *Milton Studies IX* (1976), 221–241.

724 PRINCE, F. T. "Lycidas." *The Italian Element in Milton's Verse* (**634**), pp. 71–88. [Partially reprinted in **493**.]

725 RAJAN, Balachandra. *"Lycidas:* The Shattering of the Leaves." *SP,* 64 (1967), 51–64. [Reprinted in **552**.]

726 RANSOM, John Crowe. "A Poem Nearly Anonymous." *American Review,* 1 (1933), 179–203, 444–467. [Reprinted in *The World's Body* (Scribner's, 1928), in **493**, and partially reprinted in **499**. See **697**.]

727 RIGGS, William G. "The Plant of Fame in *Lycidas.*" *Milton Studies IV* (1972), 151–161.

728 ROBINS, Harry F. "Milton's 'Two-Handed Engine at the Door' and St. Matthew's Gospel." *RES,* N.S. 5 (1954), 25–36.

729 SHUMAKER, Wayne. "Flowerets and Sounding Seas: A Study in the Affective Structure of *Lycidas.*" *PMLA,* 66 (1951), 485–494. [Reprinted in **493** and **496**.]

730 STROUP, Thomas B. *"Lycidas* and the Marinell Story." *SAMLA Studies in Milton.* Gainesville: Univ. of Florida Press, 1953, pp. 100–113.

731 THOMPSON, Claud Adelbert. " 'That Two-Handed Engine' Will Smite: Time Will Have a Stop." *SP,* 59 (1962), 184–200.

732 TUVE, Rosemond. "Theme, Pattern and Imagery in *Lycidas.*" *Images and Themes in Five Poems by Milton* (570A), pp. 73–111. [Reprinted in **493**.]

733 WALLERSTEIN, Ruth. "Iusta Edouardo King." *Studies in Seventeenth Century Poetics.* Madison: Univ. of Wisconsin Press, 1950, pp. 96–114. [Wisconsin, 1965]†

734 WILCOX, Stewart C., and RAINES, John M. *"Lycidas* and *Adonais."* *MLN,* 67 (1952), 19–21.

Miscellaneous Minor Poems

735 BALDWIN, Edward C. "Milton and the Psalms." *MP,* 17 (1919), 457–463.

736 BODDY, Margaret. "Milton's Translation of Psalms 80–88." *MP,* 64 (1966), 1–9. [Suggests that Milton's translation of these psalms had a special political application to the meeting of the Army leaders at Windsor in 1648. Also contains other biographical speculation.]

737 CAREY, John. "The Date of Milton's Italian Poems." *RES,* 14 (1963), 383–386.

737A CHAMBERS, A. B. "Milton's 'Upon the Circumcision': Backgrounds and Meanings." *TSLL,* 17 (1975), 687–697.

738 COLLETTE, Carolyn P. "Milton's Psalm Translations: Petition and Praise." *ELR,* 2 (1972), 243–259.

739 COPE, Jackson I. "Fortunate Falls as Form in Milton's 'Fair Infant.' " *JEGP,* 63 (1964), 660–674. [Following Barker (**594**), argues that the pattern is already present in "Fair Infant." Milton sees himself as a "vessel of the word" called to prophetic poetry dedicated to annunciating the resurrection.]

740 DEMARAY, John G. " 'Arcades' as a Literary Entertainment." *Papers on Language and Literature,* 8 (1972), 15–26.

741 EVANS, G. Blakemore. "Milton and the Hobson Poems." *MLQ,* 4 (1943), 281–290.

742 FREEDMAN, Morris. "Milton's 'On Shakespeare' and Henry Lawes." *SQ,* 14 (1963), 279–281.

743 HARDISON, O. B., Jr. "Milton's 'On Time' and Its Scholastic Background." *TSLL,* 3 (1961), 107–122.

744 HUNTER, William B., Jr. "Milton Translated the Psalms." *PQ,* 40 (1961), 485–494.

745 JONES, William M. "Immortality in Two of Milton's Elegies." *Myth and Symbol: Critical Approaches and Applications.* Ed. Bernice Slote. Lincoln: Univ. of Nebraska Press, 1963, pp. 133–140. ["On the Death of a Fair Infant Dying of a Cough" and "Epitaphium Damonis."]

746 LEISHMAN, James B. *Milton's Minor Poems.* Ed. Geoffrey Tillotson. London: Hutchinson, 1969; Pittsburgh: Univ. of Pittsburgh Press, 1971. ["L'Allegro"-"Il Penseroso." "Arcades," "Comus," and "Lycidas" receive separate chapters.]

747 MACLEAN, Hugh N. "Milton's *Fair Infant.*" *ELH,* 24 (1957), 296–305. [Reprinted in **476**.]

748 MADDISON, Carol. *Apollo and the Nine: A History of the Ode.* Baltimore: Johns Hopkins Press; London: Kegan Paul, 1960. [More useful for general background than for specific comments on particular poems.]

749 PARKER, William Riley. "Milton's 'Fair Infant.' " *TLS,* Dec. 17, 1938, p. 802.

750 PARKER, William Riley. "Milton's Hobson Poems: Some Neglected Early Texts." *MLR,* 31 (1936), 395–402.

751 ROSS, Malcolm M. "Milton and the Protestant Aesthetic: the Early Poems." *UTQ,* 17 (1948), 346–360.

752 SHAWCROSS, John T. "The Manuscript of *Arcades.*" *N&Q,* 6 (1959), 359–364.

753 STUDLEY, Marian H. "Milton and His Paraphrases of the Psalms." *PQ,* 4 (1925), 364–372.

754 WALLACE, John Malcolm. "Milton's *Arcades.*" *JEGP,* 58 (1959), 627–636. [Reprinted in **476**.]

755 WILLIAMS, R. Darby. "Two Baroque Game Poems on Grace: Herbert's 'Paradise' and Milton's 'On Time'." *Criticism,* 12 (1970), 180–194.

756 WILSON, Gayle Edward. "Decorum and Milton's 'An Epitaph on the Marchioness of Winchester'." *Milton Quarterly,* 8 (1974), 11–14.

Paradise Lost

In addition to the items cited here, a number of topics pertinent to the study of *Paradise Lost* will be found under *Special Topics* (p. 74), particularly under *Style and Imagery* (p. 77), *Sources, Analogues, and Comparative Studies* (p. 79), *Religion and Philosophy* (p. 85), and *Illustrations, Iconography, and Pictorial Traditions* (p. 92.).

757 ADDISON, Joseph. "Critique of *Paradise Lost.*" *Spectator,* 31 December 1711, 5 January to 3 May 1712. Reprinted in *Addison: Criticisms on Paradise Lost,* Ed. Albert S. Cook (Ginn, 1892) and in **499.**

758 ALLEN, Don Cameron. "Description as Cosmos: The Visual Image in *Paradise Lost.*" *The Harmonious Vision* (501), pp. 95–109.

759 ALLEN, Don Cameron. "Milton and the Love of Angels." *MLN,* 76 (1961), 489–490.

760 BABB, Lawrence, *The Moral Cosmos of Paradise Lost.* East Lansing: Michigan State Univ. Press, 1970.

761 BARKER, Arthur E. " 'Paradise Lost': The Relevance of Regeneration." *Paradise Lost: A Tercentenary Tribute.* Ed. B. Rajan (494), pp. 48–78.

762 BARKER, Arthur E., "Structural Pattern in *Paradise Lost.*" *PQ,* 28 (1949), 16–30. *Reprinted in 476.]*

762A BARUCH, Franklin B. "Milton's Blindness: Conscious and Unconscious Patterns of Autobiography." *ELH,* 42 (1975), 26–37.

763 BELL, Millicent. "The Fallacy of the Fall in *Paradise Lost.*" *PMLA,* 68, (1953), 863–883.

764 BELL, Millicent. "The Fallacy of the Fall in *Paradise Lost.*" *PMLA,* 70 (1955), 1187–1197, 1202–1203. [A discussion with Wayne Shumaker.]

765 BEREK, Peter. " 'Plain' and 'Ornate' Styles and the Structure of *Paradise Lost.*" *PMLA,* 85 (1970), 237–246.

766 BERGER, Harry. "*Paradise Lost* Evolving: Books I-VI." *The Centenial Review,* 11 (1967), 483–531.

767 BERRY, Boyd M. "Puritan Soldiers in *Paradise Lost.*" *MLQ,* 35 (1974), 376–402.

767A BERRY, Boyd M. *Process of Speech: Puritan Religious Writing and Paradise Lost.* Baltimore and London: Johns Hopkins Univ. Press, 1976.

768 BIRRELL, T. A. "The Figure of Satan in Milton and Blake." *Satan.* Ed. Bruno de Jésus-Marie, O.C.D. London: Sheed & Ward, 1951, pp. 379–393.

769 BLACKBURN, Thomas H. "Paradises Lost and Found: The Meaning and Function of the 'Paradise Within' in *Paradise Lost.*" *Milton Studies V* (1973), 191–211.

770 BLACKBURN, Thomas H. " 'Uncloister'd Virtue': Adam and Eve in Milton's Paradise." *Milton Studies III* (1971), 119–137.

771 BODKIN, Maud. *Archetypal Patterns in Poetry: Psychological Studies of Imagination.* London: Oxford Univ. Press; Milford, 1934. [Oxford]† [Discusses Paradise-Hades pattern, Plato's Phaedo myth, the image of woman, and Satan as devil and hero.]

772 BONHAM, Sister M. Hilda, I. H. M. "The Anthropomorphic God of *Paradise Lost.*" *PMASAL,* 53 (1968), 329–335.

773 BOWRA, C. M. *From Virgil to Milton.* London: Macmillan, 1945. [Macmillan Papermac]† [Virgil, Camões, Tasso, and Milton as representative types.]

774 BOYETTE, Purvis E. *Milton and the Sacred Fire: Sex Symbolism in Paradise Lost.* Vol. V in *Literary Monographs,* ed. Eric Rothstein. Madison: Univ. of Wisconsin Press, 1973, pp. 63–138.

775 BROADBENT, J. B. "Milton's Hell." *ELH,* 21 (1954), 161–192.

776 BROADBENT, J. B. "Milton's 'Mortal Voice' and his 'Omnific Word'." *Approaches to Paradise Lost: The York Tercentenary Lectures.* Ed. C. A. Patrides **(491)**, pp. 99–117.

777 BROADBENT, J. B. *Some Graver Subject: An Essay on Paradise Lost.* London: Chatto & Windus, 1960. [Ch. 4, "Heaven," is reprinted, with minor changes, in **492.**]

777A BRODWIN, Leonora Leet. "The Dissolution of Satan in *Paradise Lost:* A Study of Milton's Heretical Eschatology." *Milton Studies VIII* (1975), 165–207.

778 BROOKE-ROSE, Christine. "Metaphor in *Paradise Lost:* A Grammatical Analysis." *Language and Style in Milton.* Ed. Ronald D. Emma and John T. Shawcross **(482)**, pp. 252–303.

779 BROOKS, Cleanth. "Eve's Awakening." *Essays in Honor of W. C. Curry.* Nashville: Vanderbilt Univ. Press, 1954, pp. 281–298. [Reprinted in *A Shaping Joy* (Harcourt, Brace, Jovanovich, 1971) and in **496.**]

780 BUDICK, Sanford. *"Paradise Lost." Poetry of Civilization* **(507)**, pp. 57–80. [Milton's "resurrection" and renovation of Classical and Hebraic myth in *PL.*]

781 BUNDY, Murray W. "Milton's View of Education in *Paradise Lost.*" *JEGP,* 21 (1922), 127–152.

782 BURDEN, Dennis H. *The Logical Epic: A Study of the Argument of Paradise Lost.* Cambridge: Harvard Univ. Press; London: Routledge & Kegan Paul, 1967.

783 BUSH, Douglas. *Paradise Lost in Our Time: Some Comments.* Ithaca: Cornell Univ. Press; London: Milford, 1945. [Reprinted, New York: Peter Smith, 1948; 1957. Chs. reprinted in **476, 489** and **492.**]

784 BUTLER, A. Z. "The Pathetic Fallacy in *Paradise Lost.*" *Essays in Honor of Walter Clyde Curry.* Nashville: Vanderbilt Univ. Press, 1954, pp. 269–279.

785 CHAMBERS, A. B. "Chaos in *Paradise Lost.*" *JHI,* 24 (1963), 55–84.

786 CHAMBERS, A. B. "The Falls of Adam and Eve in *Paradise Lost.*" *New Essays on Paradise Lost.* Ed. Thomas Kranidas **(487)**, pp. 118–130.

787 CHAMBERS, A. B. "Milton's Proteus and Satan's Visit to the Sun." *JEGP,* 62 (1963), 280–287.

788 CHAMBERS, A. B. " 'Sin' and 'Sign' in *Paradise Lost.*" *HLQ,* 26 (1963), 381–382.

789 CHINOL, Elio. *Il Dramma Divino e il Dramma Umano nel* Paradiso Perduto. Napoli: Instituto Editoriale del Mezzo-giorno, 1958.

790 CHRISTOPHER, Georgia. "The Verbal Gate to Paradise: Adam's 'Literary Experience' in Book X of *Paradise Lost.*" *PMLA,* 90 (1975), 69–77. [See the response by Jeanne Clayton Hunter and the author's reply in *PMLA,* 91 (1976), 115–117.]

791 CIRILLO, Albert R. " 'Hail Holy Light' and Divine Time in *Paradise Lost.*"
JEGP, 68 (1969), 45–56.

792 CIRILLO, Albert R. "Noon-Midnight and the Temporal Structure of *Paradise
Lost.*" *ELH,* 29 (1962), 372–395. [Reprinted in **479** and in **492.**]

792A CLARK, Mili N. "The Mechanics of Creation: Non-contradiction and Natural
Necessity in *Paradise Lost.*" *ELR,* 7 (1977), 207–242.

793 COFFIN, Charles Monroe. "Creation and the Self in *Paradise Lost.*" Ed. C. A.
Patrides. *ELH,* 29 (1962), 1–18.

794 COHEN, Kitty. "Milton's God in Council and War." *Milton Studies III* (1971),
159–184. [Milton's God in *PL,* with emphasis on Old Testament analogues.]

795 COLIE, Rosalie. "Time and Eternity: Paradox and Structure in *Paradise Lost.*"
JWCI, 23 (1960), 127–138. [Reprinted in **66** and in **496.**]

796 COLLETT, Jonathan. "Milton's Use of Classical Mythology in *Paradise Lost.*"
PMLA, 85 (1970), 88–96.

797 COLLIER, John. *Milton's Paradise Lost: Screenplay for Cinema of the Mind.* New
York: Knopf, 1973.†

798 CONDEE, Ralph W. *Milton's Theories Concerning Epic Poetry: Their Sources and
Their Influence on* Paradise Lost. Urbana: Univ. Of Illinois Press, 1949.

799 COOK, Albert S., ed. *Addison: Criticisms on Paradise Lost.* Boston, New York,
Chicago, London: Ginn, 1892. [An edition, with index and notes, of Addison's
essays on *Paradise Lost* which appeared in the *Spectator* from Jan. 5, 1712 to May
3, 1712.]

800 COPE, Jackson I. *The Metaphoric Structure of* Paradise Lost. Baltimore: The
Johns Hopkins Press, 1962.

801 COPE, Jackson I. "Time and Space as Miltonic Symbol." *ELH,* 26 (1959),
497–513.

802 CURRY, Walter Clyde. *Milton's Ontology, Cosmology, and Physics.* Lexington:
Univ. of Kentucky Press, 1957. [Kentucky, 1966]†

803 DAICHES, David. "The Opening of *Paradise Lost.*" *The Living Milton.* Ed.
Frank Kermode **(486),** pp. 55–69.

804 DANIELLS, Roy. "A Happy Rural Seat of Various View." *Paradise Lost: A
Tercentenary Tribute.* Ed. B. Rajan **(494),** pp. 3–17. [Milton's depiction of the
Garden of Eden.]

805 DARBISHIRE, Helen. *Milton's* Paradise Lost. Oxford: Oxford Univ. Press,
1951.

806 DEMARAY, Hannah Disinger. "Milton's 'Perfect' Paradise and the Landscapes
of Italy." *Milton Quarterly,* 8 (1974), 33–41.

807 DICESARE, MARIO A. "Advent'rous Song: The Texture of Milton's Epic."
Language and Style in Milton. Ed. Ronald D. Emma and John T. Shawcross
(482), pp. 1–29.

808 DICESARE, MARIO A. "*Paradise Lost* and Epic Tradition." *Milton Studies I*
(1969), 31–50.

809 DIEKHOFF, John S. "Eve, the Devil, and *Areopagitica.*" *MLQ,* 5 (1944), 429–
434.

810 DIEKHOFF, John S. *Milton's* Paradise Lost, *a Commentary on the Argument.* New York: Columbia Univ. Press; London: Oxford Univ. Press, 1946. [Reprinted, New York: Humanities Press, 1958.]

811 DONOGHUE, Denis. "God with Thunder." *Thieves of Fire.* London: Faber & Faber, 1973, pp. 33–58. [A reading of *PL* using Aeschylus's Prometheus as an analogue.]

812 DUNCAN, Edgar H. "The Natural History of Metals and Minerals in the Universe of Milton's *Paradise Lost.*" *Osiris,* 11 (1954), 386–421.

813 DUNCAN, Joseph E. "Milton's Four-in-One Hell." *HLQ,* 20 (1957), 127–136.

814 EMPSON, William. "Emotion in Words Again." *KR,* 10 (1948), 579–601. [Reprinted in *The Structure of Complex Words.* London: Chatto & Windus, 1951, pp. 101–104. Use of "all" in emotional scenes in *Paradise Lost.]*

815 EMPSON, William. *Milton's God.* London: Chatto & Windus, 1961; Norfolk, Conn.: New Directions, 1962. Rev. ed. London: Chatto & Windus, 1965. [Part of Ch. 4 is reprinted in **492.**]

816 ERSKINE, John. "The Theme of Death in *Paradise Lost.*" *PMLA,* 32 (1917), 573–582.

817 EVANS, John M. *Paradise Lost and the Genesis Tradition.* New York: Oxford Univ. Press, 1968.

818 FERRY, Anne Davidson. *Milton's Epic Voice: The Narrator in* Paradise Lost. Cambridge: Harvard Univ. Press, 1963.

819 FISH, Stanley E. "Discovery as Form in *Paradise Lost.*" *New Essays on Paradise Lost.* Ed. Thomas Kranidas **(487)**, pp. 1–14.

820 FISH, Stanley E. "Further Thoughts on Milton's Christian Reader." *Critical Quarterly,* 7 (1965), 279–284.

821 FISH, Stanley E. "The Harassed Reader in *Paradise Lost.*" *Critical Quarterly,* 7 (1965), 162–182.

822 FISH, Stanley E. *Surprised by Sin: The Reader in Paradise Lost.* London: Macmillan; New York: St. Martins, 1967. [California Paperback, 1971]† [Ch. 1, "Not so much a Teaching as an Entangling," is reprinted in **496.**]

823 FIXLER, Michael. "The Apocalypse Within *Paradise Lost.*" *New Essays on Paradise Lost.* Ed. Thomas Kranidas **(487)**, pp. 131–178.

824 FIXLER, Michael. "Milton's Passionate Epic." *Milton Studies I* (1969), 167–192. [*PL* as a devotional poem, with the invocation of Urania in Book VII seen as "a ritual gesture of exclusion."]

825 FORSYTH, P. T. "Milton's God and Milton's Satan." *Contemporary Review,* 95 (1909), 450–465.

826 FOX, Robert C. "The Allegory of Sin and Death in *Paradise Lost.*" *MLQ,* 24 (1963), 354–364. [Sin and Death represent lust and gluttony through Milton's use of allusions.]

827 FOX, Robert C. "The Character of Mammon in *Paradise Lost.*" *RES,* 13 (1962), 30–39.

828 FOX, Robert C. "The Character of Moloch in *Paradise Lost.*" *Die neueren Sprachen,* 1962, pp. 389–395.

829 FRASER, John. *"Paradise Lost,* Book ix: A Minority Opinion." *MCR,* No. 7 (1964), 22–33. [Milton taken to task for "failures of mind" which prevent the "full surrender" of the reader to the poetry.]

830 GARDNER, Helen. "Milton's 'Satan' and the Theme of Damnation in Elizabethan Tragedy." *E & S,* 1 (1948), 46–66. [Reprinted in **476** and in **831.**]

831 GARDNER, Helen. *A Reading of Paradise Lost.* Oxford: Clarendon Press, 1965.

832 GILBERT, Allan H. *On the Composition of* Paradise Lost. *A Study of the Ordering and Insertion of Material.* Chapel Hill: Univ. of North Carolina Press, 1947. [Galaxy]†

833 GILBERT, Allan H. "The Theological Basis of Satan's Rebellion and the Function of Abdiel in *Paradise Lost."* *MP,* 40 (1942), 19–42.

834 GOLDBERG, Jonathan. "Virga Iesse: Analogy, Typology, and Anagogy in a Miltonic Simile." *Milton Studies V* (1973), 177–190. [The analogy of the tree in *PL* V as a focus for some of the poem's central meanings.]

835 GOSSMAN, Ann. "The Ring Pattern: Image, Structure, and Theme in *Paradise Lost."* *SP,* 68 (1971), 326–339.

836 GRAY, J. C. "Emptiness and Fulfillment as Structural Pattern in *Paradise Lost."* *Dalhousie Review,* 53 (1973), 78–91.

837 GRIFFIN, Dustin H. "Milton's Evening." *Milton Studies VI* (1975), 259–276.

838 GROSE, Christopher. *Milton's Epic Process: Paradise Lost and Its Miltonic Background.* New Haven: Yale Univ. Press, 1973.

839 GROSE, Christopher. "Some Uses of Sensuous Immediacy in *Paradise Lost."* *HLQ,* 31 (1968), 211–222.

840 HÄGIN, Peter. *The Epic Hero and the Decline of Heroic Poetry: A Study of the Neoclassical English Epic with Special Reference to Milton's "Paradise Lost."* Bern: Francke Verlag, 1964.†

841 HALLER, William. "Order and Progress on *Paradise Lost."* *PMLA,* 35 (1920), 218–225.

842 HAMILTON, Gary D. "Milton's Defensive God: A Reappraisal." *SP,* 69 (1972), 87–100. [The Dialogue in Heaven.]

843 HAMILTON, G. Rostrevor. *Hero or Fool? A Study of Milton's Satan.* London: Allen & Unwin, 1944.

843A HAMLET, Desmond M. *One Greater Man: Justice and Damnation in Paradise Lost.* Lewisburg, Pa.: Bucknell Univ. Press; London: Associated Univ. Presses, 1976.

844 HANFORD, James Holly. "The Dramatic Element in *Paradise Lost."* *SP,* 14 (1917), 178–195. [Reprinted in **526.**]

845 HARADA, Jun. "The Mechanism of Human Reconciliation in *Paradise Lost."* *PQ,* 50 (1971), 543–552. [The reconciliation of Adam and Eve in *PL* X.]

846 HARDISON, O. B., Jr."Written Records and Truths of Spirit in *Paradise Lost."* *Milton Studies I* (1969), 147–165. [Milton's treatment of creation as an example of a spiritually understood accommodation of the Holy Scriptures.]

847 HART, Jeffrey. *"Paradise Lost* and Order." *CE,* 25 (1964), 576–582. ["There is evidence in the poem itself that associates Eden before the fall with the England of Elizabeth, and the fall itself with the break-up of that harmonious vision."]

STUDIES OF INDIVIDUAL WORKS

848 HARTMAN, Geoffrey. "Milton's Counterplot." *ELH,* 25 (1958), 1–12. [Reprinted in **476, 479, 489.**]

848A HAÜBLEIN, Ernst. "Milton's Paraphrase of Genesis: A Stylistic Reading of *Paradise Lost,* Book VII." *Milton Studies VIII* (1975), 101–125.

849 HENRY, Nathaniel H. "The Mystery of Milton's Muse." *Renaissance Papers 1967,* pp. 69–83.

850 HERBERT, Carolyn. "Comic Elements in the Scenes of Hell in *Paradise Lost.*" *Renaissance Papers 1956*, pp. 92–101.

850A HIEATT, A. Kent. "Spenser and *Paradise Lost.*" *Chaucer, Shakespeare, Milton.* Montreal and London: McGill-Queen's Univ. Press, 1975, pp. 215–245.

851 HIGGS, Elton D. "The 'Thunder' of God in *Paradise Lost.*" *Milton Quarterly,* 4 (1970), 24–27.

852 HOFFMAN, Nancy Y. "The Hard-Hearted Hell of Self-Delusion." *Milton Quarterly,* 7 (1973), 11–14. [Milton's Hell as revealed in the implications of *PL* I, 242–255.]

853 HOWARD, Leon. " 'The Invention' of Milton's 'Great Argument': A Study of the Logic of 'God's Ways to Men.' " *HLQ,* 9 (1946), 149–173.

854 HUGHES, Merritt Y. "Beyond Disobedience." *Approaches to Paradise Lost: The York Tercentenary Lectures.* Ed. C. A. Patrides (491), pp. 181–198.

855 HUGHES, Merritt Y. "Devils to Adore for Deities." *Studies in Honor of DeWitt T. Starnes.* Ed. Thomas P. Harrison, et al. Austin: Univ. of Texas Press. 1967, pp. 241–258. [Some of the traditions behind Milton's depiction of the fallen angels in the Nativity Ode and *PL.*]

856 HUGHES, Merritt Y. "Milton and the Symbol of Light." *SEL,* 4 (1964), 1–33 [Review of critical accounts of Milton's use of light and re-examination of suggested analogues. Reprinted in **529.**]

857 HUGHES, Merritt Y. "Milton's Limbo of Vanity." *Th' Upright Heart and Pure.* Ed. Amadeus P. Fiore (483), pp. 7–24.

858 HUGHES, Merritt Y. "Myself Am Hell." *MP,* 54 (1956), 80–94. [Reprinted in **529.**]

859 HUGHES, Merritt Y. "Satan and the 'Myth' of the Tyrant." *Essays in English Literature from the Renaissance to the Victorian Age Presented to A. S. P. Woodhouse.* Ed. Miller Maclure and F. W. Watt. Toronto: Univ. of Toronto Press, 1964, pp. 125–148. [Relates Milton's Satan to Plato's conception of the political process and to the various prototypes of the tyrant in history and imaginative literature. Reprinted in **529.**]

860 HUGHES, Merritt Y. " 'Satan Now Dragon Grown' (*Paradise Lost,* X, 529)." *EA,* 20 (1968), 357–369. [The Transformation Scene in *PL,* X.]

861 H[UME], P[atrick]. *Annotations on Milton's* Paradise Lost. *Wherein the Texts of Sacred Writ Relating to the Poem, are Quoted; The Parallel Places and Imitations of the Most Excellent Homer and Virgil, Cited and Compared; All the Obscure Parts Render'd in Phrases More Familiar; The Old and Obsolete Words, with Their Originals, Explain'd and Made Easie to The English Reader.* London: Jacob Tonson, 1695.

862 HUNTER, William B., Jr. "The Meaning of 'Holy Light' in *Paradise Lost* III." *MLN,* 74 (1959), 589–592. [The prologue to Book III is addressed to the Son of God.]

54

STUDIES OF INDIVIDUAL WORKS

863 HUNTER, William B., Jr., "Milton's Urania." *SEL,* 4 (1964), 35–42. [Extends Hunter's earlier notion that Milton invokes the Son of God in Book III **(862)** to the invocations in Books I, VII, and IX.]

864 HUNTER, William B., Jr. "Prophetic Dreams and Visions in *Paradise Lost.*" *MLQ,* 9 (1948), 277–285.

865 HUNTLEY, Frank L. "A Justification of Milton's 'Paradise of Fools.' " *ELH,* 21 (1954), 107–113.

865A JACOBUS, Lee, *Sudden Apprehension: Aspects of Knowledge* in *Paradise Lost.* The Hague, Paris: Mouton, 1976.

866 JONES, Putnam Fennell. "Satan and the Narrative Structure of *Paradise Lost.*" *If by Your Art: Testament to Percival Hunt.* Ed. Agnes Lynch Starrett. Pittsburgh: Univ. of Pittsburgh Press, 1948, pp. 15–26.

867 KASTOR, Frank S. " 'By Force or Guile Eternal War': *Paradise Lost,* IV, 776–1015." *JEGP,* 70 (1971), 269–278.

868 KASTOR, Frank S. " 'In His Own Shape': The Stature of Satan in *Paradise Lost.*" *ELN,* 5 (1968), 264–269.

869 KASTOR, Frank S. "Milton's Tempter: A Genesis of a Subportrait in *Paradise Lost.*" *HLQ,* 33 (1970), 373–385. [Analogues to Satan in his role as tempter, which is seen as distinct from his other roles in *PL,* i.e., as a "subportrait."]

870 KERMODE, Frank. "Adam Unparadised." *The Living Milton.* Ed. Frank Kermode **(486),** pp. 85–123.

871 KNIGHT, Douglas. "The Dramatic Center of *Paradise Lost.*" *SAQ,* 63 (1964), 44–59.

872 KNOTT, John R., Jr. *Milton's Pastoral Vision: An Approach to Paradise Lost.* Chicago and London: Univ. of Chicago Press, 1971.

873 KRANIDAS, Thomas. "Adam and Eve in the Garden: A Study of *Paradise Lost, Book* v." *SEL,* 4 (1964), 71–83. [Milton's concept of decorum permits humanity and humor in the Christian epic. Thus the breakfast scene is "domestic, 'middle-class' comic, and still closely and clearly related to the whole."

873A LABRIOLA, Albert C. "The Aesthetics of Self-Diminution: Christian Iconography and *Paradise Lost.*" *Milton Studies VII* (1975), 267–311.

874 LANGTON, Edward. *Satan, A Portrait: A Study of Satan through All the Ages.* London: Skeffington, 1946; New York: Macmillan, 1947.

875 LAWRY, Jon S. "Reading *Paradise Lost.*" *CE,* 25 (1964), 582–586. [Structural schematization, based on the "human choice of good or evil," for use in teaching students to grasp the whole poem.]

876 LEWALSKI, Barbara Kiefer. "Innocence and Experience in Milton's Eden." *New Essays on Paradise Lost.* Ed. Thomas Kranidas **(487),** 86–117.

877 LEWALSKI, Barbara Kiefer. "*Paradise Lost* 'Introduced' and 'Structured in Space.' " *MP,* 61 (1963), 122–126.

878 LEWALSKI, Barbara Kiefer. "Structure and the Symbolism of Vision in Michael's Prophecy, *Paradise Lost,* Books XI-XII." *PQ,* 42 (1963), 25–35. [The vision cures intemperance and vainglory resulting in blindness; the spoken prophecy cures the ambition to see too much.]

55

STUDIES OF INDIVIDUAL WORKS

879 LEWIS, C. S. *A Preface to Paradise Lost.* London: Oxford Univ. Press, 1942. [Galaxy]† [Chs. VII and VIII, "The Style of the Secondary Epic" and "Defence of This Style," reprinted in **489** and in **499**; Ch. XIII, "Satan," reprinted in **476.**]

880 LIEB, Michael. *The Dialectics of Creation: Patterns of Birth and Regeneration in Paradise Lost.* Amherst: Univ. of Mass. Press, 1970.

880A LIEB, Michael. " 'Holy Place': A Reading of *Paradise Lost.*" *SEL,* 17 (1977), 129–147.

880B LIEB, Michael. "*Paradise Lost* and the Myth of Prohibition." *Milton Studies VII* (1975), 233–265.

881 LINDENBAUM, Peter. "Lovemaking in Milton's Paradise." *Milton Studies VI* (1975), 277–306.

882 LODGE, Ann. "Satan's Symbolic Syndrome: A Psychological Interpretation of Milton's Satan." *Psychoanalytic Review,* 43 (1956), 411–422. [Satan a "classical case of paranoia" depicted in highly abstracted form.]

883 LOVEJOY, Arthur O. "Milton and the Paradox of the Fortunate Fall." *ELH,* 4 (1937), 161–179. Reprinted in *Essays in the History of Ideas.* Baltimore: Johns Hopkins Press, 1948 [Capricorn, 1960]†. [Also reprinted in **479** and in **492.**]

884 LOVEJOY, Arthur O. "Milton's Dialogue on Astronomy." *Reason and the Imagination: Studies in the History of Ideas, 1600–1800.* Ed. J. A. Mazzeo. New York: Columbia Univ. Press, 1962, pp. 129–142.

885 LOW, Anthony. "Angels and Food in *Paradise Lost.*" *Milton Studies I* (1969), 135–145.

886 LOW, Anthony. "The Image of the Tower in *Paradise Lost.*" *SEL,* 10 (1970), 171–181.

887 LOW, Anthony. "Milton's God: Authority in *Paradise Lost.*" *Milton Studies IV* (1972), 19–38.

888 LOW, Anthony. "The Parting in the Garden in *Paradise Lost.*" *PQ,* 47 (1968), 30–35.

889 MACCAFFREY, Isabel Gamble. *Paradise Lost as "Myth."* Cambridge, Mass.: Harvard Univ. Press, 1959.

890 MACCAFFREY, Isabel G. "The Theme of *Paradise Lost,* Book III." *New Essays on Paradise Lost.* Ed. Thomas Kranidas (**487**), pp. 58–85.

891 MACCALLUM, H. R. "Milton and Sacred History: Books XI and XII of *Paradise Lost.*" *Essays in English Literature from the Renaissance to the Victorian Age Presented to A. S. P. Woodhouse.* Ed. Millar Maclure and F. W. Watt. Toronto: Univ. of Toronto Press, 1964, pp. 149–168. [Analyzes Milton's success in reconciling authority of sacred truth with demands of art in the review of human history.]

891A MCCANLES, Michael. "*Paradise Lost* and the Dialectic of Providence." *Dialectical Criticism and Renaissance Literature.* Berkeley, Los Angeles, London: Univ. of California Press, 1975, pp. 120–155.

892 MCCOLLEY, Diane K. "Free Will and Obedience in the Separation Scene of *Paradise Lost.*" *SEL,* 12 (1972), 103–120.

892A MCCOLLEY, Diane K. "The Voice of the Destroyer in Adam's Diatribes." *MP,* 75 (1977), 18–28. [Adam's diatribes against Eve in *PL* IX, X.]

893 MCCOLLEY, Grant. *Paradise Lost: An Account of Its Growth and Major Origins, with a Discussion of Milton's Use of Sources and Literary Patterns.* Chicago: Packard, 1940. Reprinted 1963.

894 MCCOWN, Gary M. "Milton and the Epic Epithalamium." *Milton Studies V* (1973), 39–66. [Milton's adaptation of epithalamic traditions in *PL* IV, IX, XI.]

895 MCQUEEN, William A. " 'The Hateful Siege of Contraries': Satan's Interior Monologues in *Paradise Lost."* *Milton Quarterly,* 4 (1970), 60–65.

896 MCQUEEN, William A. *"Paradise Lost* V, VI: The War in Heaven." *SP,* 71 (1974), 89–104.

897 MCQUEEN, William A. "Point of View in *Paradise Lost:* Books I-IV." *Renaissance Papers 1967.* pp. 85–92.

898 MARILLA, Esmond L. *The Central Problem of* Paradise Lost: *The Fall of Man.* Cambridge: Harvard Univ. Press, 1953.

899 MARILLA, Esmond L. "Milton's Pandemonium." *Die neueren Sprachen,* 1960, pp. 167–174.

900 MARTZ, Louis L. *"Paradise Lost:* The Journey of the Mind," *The Paradise Within: Studies in Vaughan, Traherne, and Milton.* New Haven and London: Yale Univ. Press, 1964, pp. 105–167.†

901 MARTZ, Louis L. *"Paradise Lost:* The Realms of Light." *ELR,* 1 (1971), 71–88. [Primarily a discussion of the relationship of *PL* I-II to *PL* III-IV.]

901A MILLER, George E. "Stylistic Rhetoric and the Language of God in *Paradise Lost,* Book III." *Language and Style,* 8(1975), 111–126.

902 MILLER, Milton. *"Paradise Lost:* The Double Standard." *UTQ,* 20 (1951), 183–199.

903 MINER, Earl. *"Felix Culpa* in the Redemptive Order of *Paradise Lost."* *PQ,* 47 (1968), 43–54.

904 MOHL, Ruth. "The Theme of *Paradise Lost."* *Studies in Spenser, Milton and the Theory of Monarchy.* New York: Columbia Univ. Press, 1949, pp. 66–93.

905 MOORE, C. A. "The Conclusion of *Paradise Lost."* *PMLA,* 36 (1921), 1–34.

906 MORE, Paul Elmer. "The True Theme of *Paradise Lost."* *Shelburne Essays.* (4th Ser.) London: Putnam's, 1907, pp. 239–253.

906A MURRIN, Michael. "The Language of Milton's Heaven." *MP,* 74 (1977), 350–365.

907 MUSGROVE, S. "Is the Devil an Ass?" *RES,* 21 (1945), 302–315.

908 NEWTON, J. M. "A Speculation about Landscape." *The Cambridge Quarterly,* 4 (1969), 273–282.

909 NICOLSON, Marjorie Hope. "The Telescope and Imagination." *MP,* 32 (1935), 233–260.

910 OGDEN, H. V. S. "The Crisis of *Paradise Lost* Reconsidered." *PQ,* 36 (1957), 1–19. [Reprinted in **476.**]

910A ONG, Walter J. "Milton's Logical Epic and Evolving Consciousness." *PAPS,* 120 (1976), 295–305. [Epithets in *PL* viewed within the historical context of the shift from oral to written modes of presentation.]

STUDIES OF INDIVIDUAL WORKS

911 ORAS, Ants. "Darkness Visible—Notes on Milton's Descriptive Procedures in *Paradise Lost.*" *All These To Teach: Essays in Honor of C. A. Robertson.* Ed. Robert A. Bryan et al. Gainesville: Univ. of Florida Press, 1965, pp. 130–143.

912 PARISH, John E. "Milton and the Well-fed Angel." *EM*, 18 (1967), 87–109. [Raphael: *PL* V, 219–576.]

913 PATERSON, James. *A Complete Commentary, with Etymological, Explanatory, Critical and Classical Notes on Milton's* Paradise Lost. London: R. Walker, 1744.

913A PATRICK, J. Max. "A Reconsideration of the Fall of Eve." *EA*, 28 (1975), 15–21.

914 PATRICK, John M. *Milton's Conception of Sin as Developed in Paradise Lost.* Logan: Utah State Univ. Press, 1960.

915 PATRIDES, C. A. "The Godhead in *Paradise Lost:* Dogma or Drama?" *JEGP*, 64 (1965), 29–34. [Unity of the Godhead not impaired by dramatic distinctions in the dialogue in Heaven.]

916 PATRIDES, C. A. "*Paradise Lost* and the Language of Theology." *Language and Style in Milton.* Ed. Ronald D. Emma and John T. Shawcross (**482**), pp. 102–120.

917 PATRIDES, C. A. "*Paradise Lost* and the Theory of Accommodation." *TSLL*, 5 (1963), 58–63. [On anthropomorphism.]

918 PECHEUX, Mother Mary Christopher, O. S. U. "The Concept of the Second Eve in *Paradise Lost.*" *PMLA*, 75 (1960), 359–366.

919 PECHEUX, Mother Mary Christopher, O. S. U. "The Second Adam and the Church in *Paradise Lost.*" *ELH*, 34 (1967), 173–187. [Reprinted in **479**.]

920 PETER, John. *A Critique of Paradise Lost.* London: Longmans; New York: Columbia Univ. Press, 1960. Reprinted by Archon, 1970. ["Reductive criticism" carried into great detail. Milton's shortcomings in style and substance put his aesthetic claims appreciably lower than Shakespeare's. Peter records his special debt to Waldock's *Paradise Lost and Its Critics.*]

921 PRINCE, F. T. "Milton and the Theatrical Sublime." *Approaches to Paradise Lost: The York Tercentenary Lectures.* Ed. C. A. Patrides (**491**), pp. 53–63.

922 PRINCE, F. T. "On the Last Two Books of *Paradise Lost.*" *E & S,* 11 (1958), 38–52. [Reprinted in 492.]

923 RADZINOWICZ, Mary Ann. " 'Man as a Probationer of Immortality': *Paradise Lost* XI-XII." *Approaches to Paradise Lost: The York Tercentenary Lectures.* Ed. C. A. Patrides (491), pp. 31–51.

924 RAJAN, Balachandra. "*Paradise Lost* and the Balance of Structures." *UTQ,* 41 (1972), 219–226.

925 RAJAN, Balachandra. *Paradise Lost & the Seventeenth Century Reader.* London: Chatto & Windus, 1962. [First published in 1947.]

926 RAJAN, Balachandra. "*Paradise Lost:* The Hill of History," *HLQ,* 31 (1967), 43–63. [Reprinted in **552**.]

927 RAJAN, Balachandra. "*Paradise Lost:* The Providence of Style." *Milton Studies I* (1969), 1–14. [Reprinted in **552**.]

928 RAJAN, Balachandra. " 'Paradise Lost': The Web of Responsibility." *Paradise Lost: A Tercentenary Tribute.* Ed. B. Rajan (**494**), pp. 106–140. [The intricate structure of *PL* is described as a web, whose center lies in the implications of III, 99, "Sufficient to have stood, though free to fall."]

STUDIES OF INDIVIDUAL WORKS

929 RANSOM, John Crowe. "The Idea of a Literary Anthropologist and What He Might Say of the *Paradise Lost* of Milton." *KR*, 21 (1959), 121–140.

930 REBHORN, Wayne A. "The Humanist Tradition and Milton's Satan: The Conservative as Revolutionary." *SEL*, 13 (1973), 81–93.

931 REVARD, Stella P. "The Dramatic Function of the Son in *Paradise Lost*: A Commentary on Milton's 'Trinitarianism'." *JEGP*, 66 (1967), 45–58.

932 REVARD, Stella P. "Eve and the Doctrine of Responsibility in *Paradise Lost*." *PMLA*, 88 (1973), 69–78.

933 REVARD, Stella P. "Milton's Critique of Heroic Warfare in *Paradise Lost* V and VI." *SEL*, 7 (1967), 119–139.

934 REVARD, Stella P. "Satan's Envy of the Kingship of the Son of God: A Reconsideration of *Paradise Lost*, Book 5, and Its Theological Background." *MP*, 70 (1973), 190–198.

934A REVARD, Stella P. "Vision and Revision: A Study of *Paradise Lost* 11 and *Paradise Regained*." *Papers on Language and Literature*, 10 (1974), 353–362.

935 REVARD, Stella P. "The Warring Saints and the Dragon: A Commentary Upon Revelation 12: 7–9 and Milton's War in Heaven." *PQ*, 53 (1974), 181–194.

936 RICHARDSON, J., Sr., and RICHARDSON, J., Jr. *Explanatory Notes and Remarks on Milton's* Paradise Lost. . . . *With the Life of the Author, and a Discourse on the Poem*. London: Knapton, 1734. [Partially reprinted in **499**.]

937 RICKS, Christopher. *Milton's Grand Style*. Oxford: Oxford Univ. Press, 1963. [Oxford, 1967]† [Ch. 3, "Enhancing Suggestions," is partially reprinted in **492**.]

938 RIGGS, William G. *The Christian Poet in Paradise Lost*. Berkeley, Los Angeles, London: Univ. of California Press, 1972.

939 ROBINS, Harry F. "Satan's Journey: Direction in *Paradise Lost*." *JEGP*, 60 (1961), 699–711.

939A ROLLIN, Roger B. "Milton's 'I's': The Narrator and the Reader in *Paradise Lost*." *Renaissance and Modern: Essays in Honor of Edwin M. Moseley*. Ed. Murray J. Levith. Saratoga Springs, N.Y.: Skidmore College, 1976, pp. 33–55. [See **111A**.]

940 ROLLIN, Roger B. "*Paradise Lost*: Tragical-Comical-Historical-Pastoral." *Milton Studies V* (1973), 3–37.

940A ROSENBLATT, Jason P. " 'Audacious Neighborhood': Idolatry in *Paradise Lost*, Book I." *PQ*, 54 (1975), 553–568.

941 ROSENBLATT, Jason P. "Celestial Entertainment in Eden: Book V of *Paradise Lost*." *Harvard Theological Review*, 62 (1969), 411–427.

941A ROSENBLATT, Jason P. "The Mosaic Voice in *Paradise Lost*." *Milton Studies VII* (1975), 207–232.

942 ROSENBLATT, Jason P. "Structural Unity and Temporal Concordance: The War in Heaven in *Paradise Lost*." *PMLA*, 87 (1972), 31–41. [Cf. **935**.]

943 ROSS, Malcolm M. "Poetry, Belief, and *Paradise Lost*." *Poetry and Dogma: The Transfiguration of Eucharistic Symbols in Seventeenth-Century English Poetry*. New Brunswick, N.J.: Rutgers Univ. Press, 1954, pp. 205–227. [Reprinted by Octagon Books, 1969.]

944 RYKEN, Leland. *The Apocalyptic Vision in Paradise Lost.* Ithaca and London: Cornell Univ. Press, 1970. ["Apocalyptic" here is modeled on the critical terminology of Northrop Frye.]

945 RYKEN, Leland. "Milton's Dramatization of the Godhead in *Paradise Lost.*" *Milton Quarterly,* 9 (1975), 1–6.

946 SAMUEL, Irene. "The Dialogue in Heaven: A Reconsideration of *Paradise Lost,* III. 1–417." *PMLA,* 72 (1957), 601–611. [Reprinted in **476.**]

947 SAMUEL, Irene. "Paradise Lost as Mimesis." *Approaches to Paradise Lost: The York Tercentenary Lectures.* Ed. C. A. Patrides **(491),** pp. 15–29.

948 SAMUEL, Irene. "*Purgatorio* and the Dream of Eve." *JEGP,* 63 (1964), 441–449. [Links pattern of Eve's dream to Dante's first dream on Mt. Purgatory; references to many discussions of Eve's dream.]

949 SASEK, Lawrence A. "The Drama of *Paradise Lost,* Books XI and XII." *Studies in English Renaissance Literature.* Ed. Waldo F. McNeir. Baton Rouge: Louisiana State Univ. Press, 1962, pp. 181–196. [Reprinted in **476** and in **496.**]

950 SASEK, Lawrence A. "Milton's Patriotic Epic." *HLQ,* 20 (1956), 1–14.

950A SHACKLEE, Margaret. "Grammatical Agency and the Argument for Responsibility in *Paradise Lost. ELH,* 42 (1975), 518–530.

951 SHELLEY, Percy Bysshe. "Essay on the Devil and Devils." [Written 1819? First published in] *The Works of Percy Bysshe Shelley in Verse and Prose.* Ed. Harry Buxton Forman. 8 vols. London: Reeves & Turner, 1880, VI, 382–406.

951A SHERRY, Beverley. "Speech in *Paradise Lost.*" *Milton Studies VIII* (1975), 247–266.

952 SHUMAKER, Wayne. "The Fallacy of the Fall in *Paradise Lost.*" *PMLA,* 70 (1955), 1185–1187, 1197–1202. [A discussion with Millicent Bell.]

953 SHUMAKER, Wayne. "*Paradise Lost* and the Italian Epic Tradition." *Th' Upright Heart and Pure.* Ed. Amadeus P. Fiore **(483),** pp. 87–100.

954 SHUMAKER, Wayne. *Unpremeditated Verse: Feeling and Perception in Paradise Lost.* Princeton: Princeton Univ. Press, 1967.

955 SIRLUCK, Ernest. *Paradise Lost: A Deliberate Epic.* Cambridge, Eng.: W. Heffer, 1967. [A lecture given at Churchill College, Cambridge, in 1966. 30 pages.]

955A SMITH, Eric. "*Paradise Lost.*" *Some Versions of the Fall.* Chatham, England: Univ. of Pittsburg Press, 1973, pp. 21–66.

956 SMITH, Hallett. "No Middle Flight." *HLQ,* 15 (1952), 159–172.

957 SPENCER, T. J. B. "*Paradise Lost:* The Anti-Epic." *Approaches to Paradise Lost: The York Tercentenary Lectures.* Ed. C. A. Patrides **(491),** pp. 81–98.

958 STAPLETON, Laurence. "Perspectives of Time in *Paradise Lost.*" *PQ,* 45 (1966), 734–748.

959 STEADMAN, John M. "Adam and the Prophesied Redeemer (*Paradise Lost,* XII, 359–623)." *SP,* 56 (1959), 214–225. [Reprinted in **564.**]

960 STEADMAN, John W. "Allegory and Verisimilitude in *Paradise Lost:* The Problem of the 'Impossible Credible'." *PMLA,* 78 (1963), 36–39.

961 STEADMAN, John M. "Archangel to Devil: The Background of Satan's Metamorphosis." *MLQ,* 21 (1960), 321–335. [Reprinted in **564.**]

STUDIES OF INDIVIDUAL WORKS

962 STEADMAN, John M. "Demetrius, Tasso, and Stylistic Variations in *Paradise Lost.*" *ES,* 47 (1966), 329–341.

962A STEADMAN, John M. *Epic and Tragic Structure in Paradise Lost.* Chicago: Univ. of Chicago Press, 1976.

963 STEADMAN, John M. "*Ethos* and *Dianoia:* Character and Rhetoric in *Paradise Lost.*" *Language and Style in Paradise Lost.* Ed. Ronald D. Emma and John T. Shawcross (**482**), pp. 193–232.

963A STEADMAN, John M. "The Idea of Satan, as the Hero of *Paradise Lost.*" *PAPS,* 120 (1976), 253–294.

964 STEADMAN, John M. *The Lamb and the Elephant* (**167**), pp. 88–96. [Sin and Death.]

965 STEADMAN, John M. "Mimesis and Idea: *Paradise Lost* and the Seventeenth-Century World-View." *EUQ,* 20 (1964), 67–80.

966 STEADMAN, John M. "Pandaemonium and Deliberative Oratory." *Neophil.,* 48 (1964), 159–175. [Examines the "rhetorical force" of the arguments of the fallen angels. The arguments of each are "rhetorical proofs and sophistries designed to win or seduce his companions to accept the policy most congenial to his own temperament."] [Reprinted in **564.**]

967 STEADMAN, John M. "*Paradise Lost* and the Misery of the Human Condition." *Archiv Für das Studium der Neueren Sprachen und Literaturen,* 209 (1972), 283–309.

968 STEIN, Arnold. *Answerable Style: Essays on Paradise Lost.* Minneapolis: Univ. of Minnesota Press, 1953. [Univ. of Washington]†[Chapters: "Satan," "The War in Heaven," "A Note on Hell," "The Garden," "The Fall," "Answerable Style." Ch. 2, "The War in Heaven," is reprinted in **476** and in **489**. Ch. 6, "Answerable Style," is reprinted in **492.**

968A STEIN, Arnold. *The Art of Presence: The Poet and Paradise Lost.* Berkeley, Los Angeles, London: Univ. of California Press, 1977.

969 STEIN, Arnold. "Satan's Metamorphoses: The Internal Speech." *Milton Studies I* (1969), 93–113. [Satan's internal monologues in *PL.*]

970 STOLL, Elmer Edgar. "From the Superhuman to the Human in *Paradise Lost.*" *UTQ,* 3 (1933), 3–16. [Reprinted in *From Shakespeare to Joyce.* Garden City, N.Y.: Doubleday, 1944, pp. 422–435, and in **499.**]

971 STOLL, Elmer Edgar. "Give the Devil His Due: a Reply to Mr. Lewis." *RES,* 20 (1944), 108–124.

972 STOLL, Elmer Edgar. "A Postscript to 'Give the Devil His Due.'" *PQ,* 28 (1949), 167–184.

973 STOLL, Elmer Edgar. "Was Paradise Well Lost?" *PMLA,* 33 (1918), 429–435.

974 SUMMERS, Joseph H. "The Embarrassments of *Paradise Lost.*" *Approaches to Paradise Lost: The York Tercentenary Lectures.* Ed. C. A. Patrides (**491**), pp. 65–79.

975 SUMMERS, Joseph H. *The Muse's Method: An Introduction to Paradise Lost.* Cambridge: Harvard Univ. Press; London: Chatto & Windus, 1962. [Norton, 1968]† [Ch. 8, "The Final Vision," is reprinted in **489;** Ch. 5, "The Pattern at the Center," is reprinted in **492.**]

976 SVENDSEN, Kester. "Epic Address and Reference and the Principle of Decorum in *Paradise Lost.*" *PQ,* 28 (1949), 185–206.

977   SWAIM, Kathleen M. "Flower, Fruit, and Seed: A Reading of *Paradise Lost.*" *Milton Studies V* (1973), 155–176. [The metaphorical implications of vegetation imagery in *PL*.]

977A SWAIM, Kathleen M. " 'He for God only: Shee for God in Him': Structural Parallelism in *Paradise Lost.*" *Milton Studies IX* (1976), 121–149.

978   THOMPSON, Elbert N. S. "The Theme of *Paradise Lost.*" *PMLA,* 28 (1913), 106–120.

979   TILLYARD, E. M. W. "Adam and Eve in Paradise." *Studies in Milton* **(569)**, pp. 67–70.

980   TILLYARD, E. M. W. "The Causeway from Hell to the World in the Tenth Book of *Paradise Lost.*" *SP,* 38 (1941), 266–270.

981   TILLYARD, E. M. W. "The Crisis of *Paradise Lost.*" *Studies in Milton* (569), pp. 8–52. [Reprinted in **489.**]

982   TILLYARD, E. M. W. "Milton." *The English Epic and Its Background* **(175),** pp. 430–447. [A discussion of *PL. PR* is excluded.]

983   TILLYARD, E. M. W. "A Note on Satan." *Studies in Milton* **(569),** pp. 53–61.

984   TILLYARD, E. M. W. "On Annotating *Paradise Lost,* Books IX and X." *JEGP,* 60 (1961), 808–816.

985   TILLYARD, E. M. W. "Satan, Gabriel and the Plowman." *Studies in Milton* **569),** 62–66.

986   TOLIVER, Harold E. "Complicity of Voice in *Paradise Lost.*" *MLQ,* 25 (1964), 153–170. [The various styles of *PL* and Milton's effort to move toward "a human decorum that encompasses the range of fallen experience."]

986A TOLIVER, Harold E. "Milton's Household Epic." *Milton Studies IX* (1976), 105–120.

987   VAN DOREN, Mark. *"Paradise Lost." The Noble Voice: A Study of Ten Great Poems.* New York: Holt, 1946, pp. 122–147.

988   WADDINGTON, Raymond B. "Appearance and Reality in Satan's Disguises," *TSLL,* 4 (1962), 390–398.

989   WADDINGTON, Raymond B. "The Death of Adam: Vision and Voice in Books XI and XII of *Paradise Lost.*" *MP,* 70 (1972), 9–21. [Considers the reasons for the shift from vision to narrative in *PL* XI-XII. Some interesting comments on the death of Adam, p. 15 ff.]

990   WALDOCK, A. J. A. *Paradise Lost and Its Critics.* Cambridge: Cambridge Univ. Press, 1947. [Cambridge Univ.]† [Ch. 4, "Satan and the Technique of Degradation," is reprinted in **489;** Ch. 3, "The Fall (II)," is partially reprinted in **492.** Reprinted in its entirety by Peter Smith.]

990A WANAMAKER, Melissa C. "John Milton: Opposites and Multiplicity Resolved." *Discordia Concors: The Wit of Metaphysical Poetry.* Port Washington, N.Y., London: Kennikat Press, 1975, pp. 98–124. [Relates the similes in *PL* to the concept of *discordia concors.]*

991   [WARBURTON, William.] [Notes on the first three books of *Paradise Lost.]* *History of the Works of the Learned.* April, 1740, pp. 273–280.

992   WATSON, J. R. "Divine Providence and the Structure of *Paradise Lost.*" *EC,* 14 (1964), 148–155.

993 WERBLOWSKY, R. J. Zwi. *Lucifer and Prometheus: A Study of Milton's Satan.* Introduction by C. G. Jung. London: Routledge, 1952.

994 WHALER, James. "The Miltonic Simile." *PMLA,* 46 (1931), 1034–1074.

995 WHEELER, Thomas. *Paradise Lost and the Modern Reader.* Athens: Univ. Of Georgia Press, 1974.

996 WHITING, George W. "Abdiel and the Prophet Abdias." *SP,* 60 (1963), 214–226.

997 WHITING, George W. " 'And Without Thorn the Rose.' " *Res,* 10 (1959), 60–62.

998 WHITING, George W. *Milton and This Pendant World.* Austin: Univ. of Texas Press, 1958. [Reprinted by Octagon Books, 1969.]

999 WIDMER, Kingsley. "The Iconology of Renunciation: The Miltonic Simile." *ELH,* 25 (1958), 258–269. [Reprinted in **479** and in **492.**]

1000 WILDING, Michael. *Milton's Paradise Lost.* Sidney, Australia: Sidney Univ. Press, 1969.

1001 WILLIAMS, Arnold. "The Motivation of Satan's Rebellion in *Paradise Lost.* " *SP,* 42 (1945), 253–268. [Reprinted in **496.**]

1002 WILLIAMSON, George. The Education of Adam." *MP,* 61 (1963), 96–109. [Reprinted in **476** and in **575.**]

1003 WOODHOUSE, A. S. P. "Pattern in *Paradise Lost.* " *UTQ,* 22 (1953), 109–127.

1004 WRIGHT, B. A., *Milton's* Paradise Lost: *A Reassessment of the Poem.* London: Methuen; New York: Barnes & Noble, 1962.†

1005 ZAROV, Herbert. "Milton and the Rhetoric of Rebellion." *Milton Quarterly,* 7 (1973), 47–50. [The implications of Satan's rhetoric as opposed to God's plain style.]

Paradise Regained

In addition to the items cited below, further references pertinent to *Paradise Regained* may be found under Special Topics (p. 74), particularly under Style and Imagery (p. 77) Sources, Analogues, and Comparative Studies (p. 79), Religion and Philosophy (p. 85), and Illustrations, Iconography, and Pictorial Traditions (p. 92).

1006 ALLEN, Don Cameron. "Realization as Climax: *Paradise Regained.* " *The Harmonious Vision* **(501),** pp. 110–124.

1007 BARKER, Arthur E. "Structural and Doctrinal Pattern in Milton's Later Poems." *Essays in English Literature from the Renaissance to the Victorian Age Presented to A. S. P. Woodhouse.* Ed. Millar MacLure and F. W. Watt. Toronto: Univ. of Toronto Press, 1964, pp. 169–194. [Applies Milton's developing doctrine of Christian liberty to his later poems.]

1007A CHAMBERS, A. B. "The Double Time Scheme in *Paradise Regained.* " *Milton Studies VII* (1975), 189–205

1008 CLARK, Ira. "Christ on the Tower in *Paradise Regained.* " *Milton Quarterly,* 8 (1974), 104–107.

STUDIES OF INDIVIDUAL WORKS

1009 CLARK, Ira. "*Paradise Regained* and the Gospel According to John." *MP,* 71 (1973), 1–15.

1010 CONDEE, Ralph W. "Milton's Dialogue with the Epic: *Paradise Regained* and the Tradition." *YR,* 59 (1970), 357–375. [Reprinted in **515.**]

1011 FINK, Zera S. "The Political Implications of *Paradise Regained.*" *JEGP,* 40 (1941), 482–488.

1012 FISH, Stanley E. "Inaction and Silence: The Reader in *Paradise Regained.*" *Calm of Mind.* Ed. Joseph Wittreich, Jr. (**500**), pp. 25–47.

1013 FIXLER, Michael. "Christ's Kingdom and *Paradise Regained.*" *Milton and the Kingdoms of God.* Evanston, Ill.: Northwestern Univ. Press, 1964, pp. 221–271.

1014 FORTIN, René E. "The Climactic Similes of *Paradise Regained:* 'True Wisdom' or 'False Resemblance.'?" *Milton Quarterly,* 7 (1973), 39–43.

1015 FRYE, Northrop. "The Typology of *Paradise Regained.*" *MP,* 53 (1956), 227–238. [Reprinted in **476, 492,** and **523.**]

1016 GILBERT, Allan H. "The Temptation in *Paradise Regained,*" *JEGP,* 15 (1916), 599–611.

1017 GUSS, Donald. "A Brief Epic: *Paradise Regained.*" *SP,* 68 (1971), 223–243.

1018 HAMILTON, Gary D. "Creating the Garden Anew: The Dynamics of *Paradise Regained.*" *PQ,* 50 (1971), 567–581.

1018A HIEATT, A. Kent. "Spenser and *Paradise Regained.*" *Chaucer, Shakespeare, Milton.* Montreal and London: McGill-Queen's Univ. Press, 1975, pp. 247–255.

1019 HUGHES, Merritt Y. "The Christ of *Paradise Regained* and the Renaissance Heroic Tradition." *SP,* 35 (1938), 254–277. [Reprinted in **529**]

1020 HUNTER, William B., Jr. "The Obedience of Christ in *Paradise Regained.*" *Calm of Mind.* . . . Ed. Joseph Wittreich, Jr. (**500**), pp. 67–75.

1020A JORDAN, Richard Douglas. "*Paradise Regained* and the Second Adam." *Milton Studies IX* (1976), 261–275.

1021 KERMODE, Frank. "Milton's Hero." *RES,* 4 (1953), 317–330.

1022 LANGFORD, Thomas. "The Temptations in *Paradise Regained.*" *TSLL,* 9 (1967), 37–46.

1023 LASKOWSKY, Henry J. "Miltonic Dialogue and the Principle of Antithesis in Book Three of *Paradise Regained.*" *Thoth,* no. 4, pp. 24–29.

1024 LEWALSKI, Barbara Kiefer. *Milton's Brief Epic: The Genre, Meaning, & Art of Paradise Regained.* Providence. Brown Univ. Press; London: Methuen, 1966.

1025 LEWALSKI, Barbara Kiefer. "Theme and Structure in *Paradise Regained.*" *SP,* 57 (1960), 186–220. [Reprinted in revised form in **492.**]

1026 LEWALSKI, Barbara Kiefer. "Time and History in *Paradise Regained.*" *The Prison and the Pinnacle.* Ed. B. Rajan (**495**), pp. 49–81.

1027 MARILLA, E. L. "*Paradise Regained:* Observations on its Meaning." *Studia Neophilologica,* 27 (1955), 179–191.

1028 MARTZ, Louis L. "*Paradise Regained:* The Interior Teacher." *The Paradise Within: Studies in Vaughan, Traherne, and Milton.* New Haven and London: Yale Univ. Press, 1964, pp. 171–201. [Revised from **1029.** Reprinted in **492.**]

1029 MARTZ, Louis L. "*Paradise Regained:* The Meditative Combat." *ELH,* 27 (1960), 223–247.

STUDIES OF INDIVIDUAL WORKS

1030 *Milton's Paradise Regained: Two Eighteenth-Century Critiques by Richard Mea-
dowcourt and Charles Dunster.* Facsimile Reproductions with an Introduction by
J. A. Wittreich, Jr. Gainesville, Florida: Scholars' Facsimiles & Reprints, 1971.

1031 ORANGE, Linwood E. "The Role of the Deadly Sins in *Paradise Regained.*"
SoQ, 2 (1964), 190–201. [Unity secured by organizing the temptations around the
Seven Deadly Sins.]

1032 PECHEUX, Mother Mary Christopher, O. S. U. "Sin in *Paradise Regained:* The
Biblical Background." *Calm of Mind.* Ed. Joseph A. Wittreich, Jr. **(500),** pp.
49–65.

1033 POPE, Elizabeth. *Paradise Regained: The Tradition and the Poem.* Baltimore:
Johns Hopkins Press, 1947. [Reprinted by Russell & Russell, 1962.]

1034 RAJAN, Balachandra. "Jerusalem and Athens: The Temptation of Learning in
'Paradise Regained'." *Th' Upright Heart and Pure.* Ed. Amadeus P. Fiore **(483)**
61–74.

1035 RANSOM, John Crowe. *God Without Thunder: An Unorthodox Defense of Orthodoxy.* New York: Harcourt, Brace, 1930. [Milton is referred to frequently in
the chapters entitled "Satan as Science" and "Christ as Science." These chapters
may prove to be helpful for readers who have difficulty in establishing rapport with
Christ in *PL* and *PR.*]

1035A REVARD, Stella. "Vision and Revision: A Study of *Paradise Lost* 11 and *Paradise Regained.*" *Papers on Language and Literature,* 10 (1974), 353–362.

1036 RICKS, Christopher. "Over-Emphasis in *Paradise Regained.*" *MLN,* 76 (1961),
701–704.

1037 SAFER, Elaine B. "The Socratic Dialogue and 'Knowledge in the Making' in
Paradise Regained." *Milton Studies VI* (1975), 215–226.

1038 SAMUEL, Irene. "The Regaining of Paradise." *The Prison and the Pinnacle.* Ed.
B. Rajan **(495),** pp. 111–134. [An argument against reading *PR* as an identity crisis
which is resolved by Christ's comprehension of his divinity in the final temptation.]

1039 SCHULTZ, Howard. "Christ and Antichrist in *Paradise Regained.*" *PMLA,* 67
(1952), 790–808.

1040 STEADMAN, John M. " 'Like Turbulencies': The Tempest of *Paradise Regain'd*
as Adversity Symbol." *MP,* 59 (1961), 81–88. [Reprinted in **564.**]

1041 STEADMAN, John M. "*Paradise Regained:* Moral Dialectic and the Pattern of
Rejection." *UTQ,* 31 (1962), 416–430. [Reprinted in **564.**]

1042 STEADMAN, John M. "The 'Tree of Life' Symbolism in *Paradise Regain'd.*"
RES, 11 (1960), 384–391. [Reprinted in **564.**]

1043 STEIN, Arnold. "*Paradise Regained.*" *Heroic Knowledge: An Interpretation of
Paradise Regained and Samson Agonistes.* Minneapolis: Univ. of Minnesota
Press, 1957, pp. 3–134. [Reprinted by Archon, 1965]

1044 SUNDELL, Roger H. "The Narrator as Interpreter in *Paradise Regained.*" *Milton Studies II* (1970), 83–101.

1045 TAYLOR, Dick, Jr. "The Storm Scene in *Paradise Regained:* A Reinterpreta-
tion." *UTQ,* 24 (1955), 359–376.

1046 TILLYARD, E. M. W. "The Christ of *Paradise Regained.*" *Studies in Milton*
(569), pp. 100–106.

1047 WILKES, G. A. *"Paradise Regained* and the Conventions of the Sacred Epic." *ES,* 44 (1963), 35–38.

1048 WITTREICH, Joseph A., Jr. "William Blake: Illustrator-Interpreter of *Paradise Regained." Calm of Mind.* Ed. Joseph Wittreich, Jr. **(500),** pp. 93–132. [Illustrated] [See **1531, 1532, 1604,**]

1049 WOODHOUSE, A. S. P. "Theme and Pattern in *Paradise Regained." UTQ,* 25 (1956), 167–182. [Reprinted in revised form in **577.**]

1050 ZWICKY, Laurie, "Kairos in *Paradise Regained:* The Divine Plan." *ELH,* 31 (1964), 271–277. ["Kairos" is the Greek and New Testament notion of a moment designated for a significant event. Satan's effort in *PR* is "to get Christ to act before his time or kairos."]

Samson Agonistes

In addition to the items cited below, further items pertinent to *Samson Agonistes* may be found under the various categories of Special Topics (pp. 74–100).

1051 ALLEN, Don Cameron. "The Idea as Pattern: Despair and *Samson Agonistes." The Harmonious Vision* **(501),** pp. 71–94. [Partially reprinted in **480.**]

1052 ARTHOS, John. "Milton and Monteverdi." *Milton and the Italian Cities.* New York: Barnes & Noble, 1968, pp. 129–205. [The Italian musical drama as a background for understanding *SA.*]

1052A ASALS, Heather. "In Defense of Dalila: *Samson Agonistes* and the Reformation Theology of the Word." *JEGP,* 74 (1975), 183–194.

1053 BARKER, Arthur E. "Structural and Doctrinal Pattern in Milton's Later Poems." *Essays in English Literature from the Renaissance to the Victorian Age Presented to A. S. P. Woodhouse.* Ed. Millar MacLure and F. W. Watt. Toronto: Univ. of Toronto Press, 1964, pp. 169–194. [Partially reprinted in **480.**]

1054 BAUMM, Paull Franklin. *"Samson Agonistes* Again." *PMLA,* 36 (1921). 354–371.

1055 BEUM, Robert. "The Rhyme in *Samson Agonistes." TSLL,* 4 (1962), 177–182.

1056 BOSWELL, Jackson Campbell. "Samson's Bosom Snake." *Milton Quarterly,* 8 (1974). 77–80.

1057 BOUGHNER, Daniel C. "Milton's Harapha and Renaissance Comedy." *ELH,* 11 (1944), 297–306.

1058 BOWRA, Sir Cecil Maurice. *"Samson Agonistes." Inspiration and Poetry.* London: Macmillan, 1955, pp. 112–129.

1059 BUDICK, Sanford. *"Samson Agonistes." Poetry of Civilization* **(507),** pp. 45–57.

1060 BURKE, Kenneth. "The Imagery of Killing." *HudR,* 1 (1948), 151–167.

1061 CHAMBERS, A. B. "Wisdom and Fortitude in *Samson Agonistes." PMLA,* 78 (1963), 315–320.

1062 CHRISTOPHER, Georgia. "Homeopathic Physic and Natural Renovation in *Samson Agonistes." ELH,* 37 (1970), 361–373.

1063 CIRILLO, Albert R. "Time, Light, and the Phoenix: The Design of *Samson Agonistes." Calm of Mind.* Ed. Joseph Wittreich, Jr. **(500),** pp. 209–233.

1064 CLARE, Sister Miriam. O. S. F. *Samson Agonistes: A Study in Contrast.* New York: Pageant Press, 1964. [Milton's use of rhetorical figures of contrast and their relationship to the drama as a whole.]

1065 COHEN, Michael. "Rhyme in *Samson Agonistes.*" *Milton Quarterly,* 8 (1974). 4–6.

1066 COX, Lee Sheridan. "The 'Ev'ning Dragon' in *Samson Agonistes:* A Reappraisal." *MLN,* 76 (1961), 577–584.

1067 COX, Lee Sheridan. "Natural Science and Figurative Design in *Samson Agonistes.*" *ELH,* 35 (1968), 51–74. [Reprinted in **479.**]

1068 CURRY, Walter Clyde. "*Samson Agonistes* Yet Again." *SR,* 32 (1924), 336–352.

1069 DANIELS, Edgar F. "Samson in *Areopagitica.*" *N&Q,* N.S. 11 (1964), 92–93.

1070 EBBS, John Dale. "Milton's Treatment of Poetic Justice in *Samson Agonistes.*" *MLQ,* 22 (1961), 377–389.

1071 ELLIS-FERMOR, Una. "*Samson Agonistes* and Religious Drama." *The Frontiers of Drama.* London: Methuen, 1945, pp. 17–33. [Reprinted in **485.**]

1072 EMPSON, William. "A Defense of Delilah." *Sewanee Review,* 68 (1960), 240–255.

1073 FELL, Kenneth, "From Myth to Martyrdom: Towards a View of Milton's *Samson Agonistes*" *ES,* 34 (1953), 145–155.

1073A FERRY, Anne Davidson. "Samson's 'Fort of Silence.' " *Milton and the Miltonic Dryden* (**1301**), pp. 127–177.

1074 FINNEY, Gretchen Ludke. "Chorus in *Samson Agonistes.*" *PMLA,* 58 (1943), 649–664.

1075 FISH, Stanley E. "Question and Answer in *Samson Agonistes.*" *Critical Quarterly,* 11 (1969), 237–264.

1076 FRYE, Northrop. "Agon and Logos: Revolution and Revelation." *The Prison and the Pinnacle.* Ed. B. Rajan (**495**), pp. 135–163. [Aspects of tragedy in *SA.*]

1077 GILBERT, Allan H. "*Is Samson Agonistes* Unfinished?" *PQ,* 28 (1949,) 98–106.

1078 GOSSMAN, Ann. "Milton's Samson as the Tragic Hero Purified by Trial." *JEGP,* 61 (1962), 528–541.

1079 GOSSMAN, Ann. "Samson, Job, and 'the Exercise of Saints.' " *ES,* 45 (1964), 212–224. [The relation of *SA* to the Book of Job.]

1080 HALLER, William. "The Tragedy of God's Englishmen." *Reason and the Imagination: Studies in the History of Ideas. 1600–1800.* Ed. J. A. Mazzeo. New York: Columbia Univ. Press; London: Routledge & Kegan Paul, 1962, pp. 201–211.

1081 HANFORD, James Holly. "*Samson Agonistes* and Milton in Old Age." *Studies in Shakespeare, Milton, and Donne.* New York: Macmillan, 1925, pp. 167–189. [Reprinted in **480, 485, 526.**]

1082 HARRIS, William O. "Despair and 'Patience as the Truest Fortitude' in *Samson Agonistes.*" *ELH,* 30 (1963), 107–120. [Reprinted in **479.**]

1083 HAWKINS, Sherman H. "Samson's Catharsis." *Milton Studies II* (1970), 211–230.

1084 HOFFMAN, Nancy Y. "Samson's Other Father: The Character of Manoa in *Samson Agonistes.*" *Milton Studies II* (1970), 195–210.

STUDIES OF INDIVIDUAL WORKS

1085 HUNTLEY, John F. "A Revaluation of the Chorus' Role in Milton's *Samson Agonistes.*" *MP,* 64 (1966), 132–145.

1086 JEBB, Sir R. C. "*Samson Agonistes* and the Hellenic Drama." *Proceedings of the British Academy.* 3 (1907–1908). 341–348. [Reprinted in **485.**]

1087 KERRIGAN, William. *The Prophetic Milton* **(533).** [Ch. 4, "Prophetic Actors," and Ch. 5, "Prophetic Time," discuss *SA* extensively.]

1088 KESSNER, Carole S. "Milton's Hebraic Herculean Hero." *Milton Studies VI* (1975), 243–258.

1089 KIRKCONNELL, Watson. *That Invincible Samson: The Theme of Samson Agonistes in World Literature with Translations of the Major Analogues.* Toronto: Univ. of Toronto Press, 1964.

1090 KROUSE, F. Michael. *Milton's Samson Agonistes and the Christian Tradition.* Princeton: Princeton Univ. Press for the Univ. of Cincinnati, 1949. [Reprinted by Shoestring Press, 1963. Five pages on "The Epithet *Agonistes*" are reprinted in **480.**]

1091 LEWALSKI, Barbara K. "*Samson Agonistes* and the 'Tragedy' of the Apocalypse." *PMLA.* 85 (1970). 1050–1062.

1092 LOW, Anthony. "Addenda to a Checklist of Criticism of *Samson Agonistes.*" *RECTR* 7, i (1968), 53–54.

1093 LOW, Anthony. *The Blaze of Noon: A Reading of Samson Agonistes.* New York and London: Columbia Univ. Press, 1974.

1094 MADSEN, William G. "Samson and Christ." *From Shadowy Types to Truth.* New Haven and London: Yale Univ. Press, 1968. pp. 181–202. [This essay was first published, in somewhat different form, in **498,** pp. 95–114. The earlier version is partially reprinted in **480.** Cf. **1117.**]

1095 MARILLA, E. L. "*Samson Agonistes:* An Interpretation." *Studia Neophilologica,* 29 (1957), 67–76.

1096 MARTZ, Louis L. "Chorus and Character in *Samson Agonistes.*" *Milton Studies I* (1969), 115–134.

1097 MUELLER, Martin E. "*Pathos* and *Katharsis* in *Samson Agonistes.*" *ELH,* 31 (1964). 156–174. [The catastrophe *(pathos)* is not in accord with Aristotle's requirement in that a teleological nexus replaces the causal nexus of probability and necessity. Reprinted in **479.**]

1098 ONUSKA, John T., Jr. "The Equation of Action and Passion in *Samson Agonistes.*" *PQ,* 52 (1973), 69–84.

1099 PARKER, William Riley. "The Date of *Samson Agonistes.*" *PQ,* 28 (1949), 145–166. [Reprinted in **485.** Cf. **1112, 466, 1239, 1231, 1107,** and **1100.**]

1100 PARKER, William Riley. "The Date of *Samson Agonistes* Again." *Calm of Mind.* Ed. Joseph Wittreich, Jr. **(500),** pp. 163–174.

1101 PARKER, William Riley. *Milton's Debt to Greek Tragedy in Samson Agonistes.* Baltimore: Johns Hopkins Univ. Press; London: Milford, 1937. [Reprinted by Archon, 1963, and by Barnes & Noble, 1968, 1970.]

1102 PARKER, William Riley. "Notes on the Text of *Samson Agonistes.*" *JEGP,* 60 (1961). 688–698.

1103 PARKER, William Riley. "The Trinity Manuscript and Milton's Plans for a Tragedy." *JEGP,* 34 (1935). 225–232.

STUDIES OF INDIVIDUAL WORKS

1104 PRICE, Reynolds. "Poem Doctrinal and Exemplary to a Nation: A Reading of *Samson Agonistes.*" *Things Themselves.* New York: Atheneum, 1972, pp. 214–259.

1105 RADZINOWICZ, Mary Ann Nevins. "Eve and Dalila: Renovation and the Hardening of the Heart." *Reason and the Imagination: Studies in the History of Ideas, 1600–1800.* Ed. J. A. Mazzeo. New York: Columbia Univ. Press; London: Routledge & Kegan Paul, 1962, pp. 155–181.

1106 RADZINOWICZ, Mary Ann Nevins. "*Samson Agonistes* and Milton the Politician in Defeat." *PQ,* 44 (1965). 454–471.

1107 RIDDEN, Geoffrey. "Milton and Phillips' *New World of Words.*" *Milton Quarterly.* 7 (1973). 29–32.

1108 SAMUEL, Irene. "*Samson Agonistes* as Tragedy." *Calm of Mind.* Ed. Joseph Wittreich, Jr. (500), pp. 235–257.

1109 SCOTT-CRAIG, T. S. K. "Concerning Milton's Samson." *RN,* 5 (1952), 45–53.

1110 SELLIN, Paul R. "Milton's Epithet *Agonistes.*" *SEL,* 4 (1964), 137–162. [Examines roots of *agonistes* and concludes that the epithet points to Samson "dissembling" as the "action" of the drama. The dissembling begins with the second entrance of the Officer.]

1111 SELLIN, Paul R. "Sources of Milton's Catharsis: A Reconsideration." *JEGP,* 60 (1961). 712–730.

1112 SIRLUCK, Ernest. "Some Recent Changes in the Chronology of Milton's Poems: *Samson Agonistes.*" *JEGP,* 60 (1961). 773–781. [Reprinted in **490**, pp. 165–173.]

1113 STEADMAN, John M. " 'Faithful Champion': The Theological Basis of Milton's Hero of Faith." *Anglia,* 77 (1959), 12–28. [Reprinted in **476** and in **564**.]

1114 STEADMAN, John M. " 'Passions Well Imitated': Rhetoric and Poetics in the Preface to *Samson Agonistes.*" *Calm of Mind.* Ed. Joseph Wittreich, Jr. (500), pp. 175–207.

1115 STEIN, Arnold. "*Samson Agonistes.*" *Heroic Knowledge: An Interpretation of Paradise Regained and Samson Agonistes* (1043), pp. 137–202. [Partially reprinted in **480**.]

1116 STOLLMAN, Samuel S. "Milton's Samson and the Jewish Tradition." *Milton Studies III* (1971), 185–200.

1117 STOLLMAN, Samuel S. "Milton's Understanding of the 'Hebraic' in *Samson Agonistes.*" *SP,* 69 (1972), 334–347.

1118 STRATMAN, Carl J. "Milton's *Samson Agonistes:* A Checklist of Criticism." *RECTR,* 4 (1965), 2–10. [See **1092**.]

1119 SUMMERS, Joseph H. "The Movements of the Drama." *The Lyric and Dramatic Milton.* Ed. Joseph H. Summers (498), pp. 153–175.

1120 THORPE, James. "On the Pronunciation of Names in *Samson Agonistes.*" *HLQ,* 31 (1967), 65–74.

1121 TINKER, Chauncey B. "*Samson Agonistes.*" *Tragic Themes in Western Literature.* Ed. Cleanth Brooks. New Haven: Yale Univ. Press, 1955, pp. 59–76.

1122 WADDINGTON, Raymond B. "Melancholy Against Melancholy: *Samson Agonistes* as Renaissance Tragedy." *Calm of Mind.* Ed. Joseph Wittreich, Jr. (500), pp. 259–287.

1123 WEISMILLER, Edward R. "The 'Dry' and 'Rugged' Verse." *The Lyric and Dramatic Milton*. Ed. Joseph H. Summers (**498**), pp. 115–152. [The prosody of the choruses of *SA* is examined against the background of some of Milton's earlier poems and the odes of Crashaw, Cowley, and the Italians.]

1124 WELCHER, Jeanne K. "The Meaning of Manoa." *Milton Quarterly*, 8 (1974), 48–50.

1125 WILKES, G. A. "The Interpretation of *Samson Agonistes.*" *HLQ*, 26 (1963), 363–379.

1126 WILKENFELD, Roger B. "Act and Emblem: The Conclusion of *Samson Agonistes.*" *ELH*, 32 (1965), 160–168.

1127 WOODHOUSE, A.S.P. "*Samson Agonistes* and Milton's Experience." *TRSC*, 3rd Ser., 43, Sec. 2 (1949). 157–175. [Reprinted in **577**.]

1128 WOODHOUSE, A. S. P. "Tragic Effect in *Samson Agonistes.*" *UTQ*, 28 (1959), 205–222. [Reprinted in **476** and in **577**.]

Prose Works

In addition to the items cited below, further works pertinent to Milton prose may be found under Special Topics (pp. 74–100) or under General Criticism (pp. 33–38).

1129 BARKER, Arthur E. "Christian Liberty in Milton's Divorce Pamphlets." *MLR*. 35 (1940), 153–161.

1130 BARKER, Arthur. *Milton and the Puritan Dilemma, 1641–1660.* Toronto: Univ. of Toronto Press; London: Milford, 1942. [Reprinted, Toronto: Univ. of Toronto Press, 1956.] [The dilemma is the failure of the Revolution to produce the society which might logically have followed from its premises. A comprehensive survey of Milton's thought in the tracts on Christian and human liberty and in the *De Doctrinia.*]

1131 BENJAMIN, Edwin B. "Milton and Tacitus." *Milton Studies IV* (1972), 117–140.

1132 BOWERS, A. Robin. "Milton and Salmasius: The Rhetorical Imperatives." *PQ*, 52 (1973), 55–68.

1132A CAMPBELL, Gordon. "*De Doctrina Christiana:* Its Structural Principles and Its Unfinished State." *Milton Studies IX* (1976), 243–260.

1132B CAMPBELL, Gordon. "Miltons Accedence Commenc't Grammar." Milton *Q*, 10 (1976), 39–48.

1133 CAWLEY, Robert R. *Milton's Literary Craftsmanship: A Study of A Brief History of Moscovia, with an Edition of the Text.* Princeton: Princeton Univ. Press 1941. [Reprinted by Gordian, 1965.]

1134 CLYDE, William M. *The Struggle for the Freedom of the Press from Caxton to Cromwell.* London, New York: H. Milford, Oxford Univ. Press for St. Andrews Univ., 1934.

1134A EGAN, James. "Milton and the Marprelate Tradition." *Milton Studies VIII* (1975), 103–121. [Discusses *Animadversions* and *Colasterion* against the background of the Marprelate tradition.]

STUDIES OF INDIVIDUAL WORKS

1135 EVANS, John X. "Imagery as Argument in Milton's *Areopagitica.*" *TSLL,* 8 (1969), 189–205.

1136 FINK, Zera S. "Immortal Government: The Free Commonwealth." *The Classical Republicans: An Essay in the Recovery of a Pattern of Thought in Seventeenth-Century England* (78), pp. 90–122. [Milton's efforts to achieve a mixed state.]

1137 FINK, Zera S. "The Theory of the Mixed State and the Development of Milton's Political Thought." *PMLA,* 57 (1942), 705–736.

1138 FIRTH, C. H. "Milton as an Historian." *Proceedings of the British Academy,* 3 (1907–1908), 227–257, [Reprinted in *Essays, Historical and Literary,* Oxford: Oxford Univ. Press, 1938, pp. 61–102. *Study of a History of Britain.*]

1139 FISH, Stanley E. "Reason in *The Reason of Church Government.*" *Self-Consuming Artifacts: The Experience of Seventeenth-Century Literature.* Berkeley, Los Angeles, London: Univ. of California Press, 1972, pp. 265–302. [California Paperback *CAL* 298, 1974.]†

1140 FISH, Stanley E. "Reasons That Imply Themselves: Imagery, Argument, and the Reader in Milton's *Reason of Church Government.*" *Seventeenth-Century Imagery: Essays on Uses of Figurative Language from Donne to Farquhar.* Ed. Earl Miner. Berkeley, Los Angeles, London: Univ. of California Press, 1971, pp. 83–102. [Reprinted in expanded form in **1139.**]

1141 FLETCHER, Harris F. *The Use of the Bible in Milton's Prose.* Urbana: Univ. of Illinois Press, 1929.

1142 FRENCH, J. Milton. "Milton as a Historian." *PMLA,* 50 (1935), 469–479.

1143 FRENCH, J. Milton. "Some Notes on Milton's *Accedence Commenc't Grammar.*" *JEGP,* 60 (1961), 641–650.

1144 GILBERT, Allan H. "Milton's Defense of Bawdry." *SAMLA Studies in Milton.* Gainesville: Univ. of Fla. Press, 1953, pp. 54–71.

1145 GILMAN, W. E. *Milton's Rhetoric: Studies in His Defense of Liberty.* Columbia: Univ. of Missouri Press, 1939.

1146 GLEASON, John B. "The Nature of Milton's *Moscovia.*" *SP,* 61 (1964), 640–649. ["The *Moscovia* as we have it represents a preparatory stage in a project which was soon abandoned."]

1147 GLICKSMAN, Harry. "The Sources of Milton's *History of Britain.*" *UWSLL,* 2 (1920), 105–144.

1148 HALLER, William. "Before *Areopagitica.*" *PMLA,* 42 (1927), 875–900. [An examination of the writings on liberty which appeared in London just before *Areopagitica.*]

1149 HAMILTON, K. G. "The Structure of Milton's Prose." *Language and Style in Milton.* Ed. Ronald D. Emma and John T. Shawcross (482), pp. 304–332.

1150 HANFORD, James Holly. "The Date of Milton's *De Doctrina Christiana.*" *SP,* 17 (1920), 309–318.

1151 HENRY, Nathaniel H. "Milton's Last Pamphlet: Theocracy and Intolerance." *A Tribute to George Coffin Taylor: Studies and Essays, Chiefly Elizabethan. by His Students and Friends.* Ed. Arnold Williams. Chapel Hill: Univ. of North Carolina Press, 1952, pp. 197–210. [On *Of True Religion.*]

STUDIES OF INDIVIDUAL WORKS

1151A HILL, Christopher. "Milton the Radical." *TLS* 29 Nov 1974, pp. 1330–1332. [For responses in *TLS,* see the following issues: 13 Dec 74, p. 1416; 10 Jan 75, p. 36; 24 Jan 75, p. 84; 31 Jan 75, p. 112; 14 Feb 75, p. 168; 24 Oct 75, pp. 1250–52; 7 Nov 75, p. 1333; 14 Nov 75, p. 1360; 28 Nov 75, p. 1419; 12 Dec 75, p. 1489.]

1152 HUGHES, Merritt Y. "New Evidence on the Charge that Milton Forged the Pamela Prayer in the *Eikon Basilike.*" *RES, N.S.* 3 (1952), 130–140.

1153 HUGUELET, Theodore L. "The Rule of Charity in Milton's Divorce Tracts." *Milton Studies VI* (1975), 199–214.

1154 HUNTER, William B, Jr. "The Theological Context of Milton's *Christian Doctrine.*" *Achievements of the Left Hand.* Ed. Michael Lieb and John T. Shawcross **(488)**, pp. 269–287.

1155 HUNTLEY, John F. "The Images of Poet and Poetry in Milton's *Reason of Church-Government.*" *Achievements of the Left Hand.* Ed. Michael Lieb and John T. Shawcross **(488)**, pp. 83–120.

1156 HUNTLEY, John F. "*Proairesis, Synteresis,* and the Ethical Orientation of Milton's *Of Education.*" *PQ,* 43 (1964), 40–46. [Milton's preference for the term "proairesis" (moral choice) over the more scholastic "synteresis" accords with his emphasis on practical and intellecutual virtues rather than Christian pieties.]

1157 KELLEY, Maurice. "Milton's Debt to Wolleb's *Compendium Theologiae Christianae.*" *PMLA,* 50 (1935), 156–165.

1158 KERRIGAN, William. "Visionary Song, Zealous Prose." *The Prophetic Milton* **(533)**, pp. 125–187. [For the prose see especially p. 163 *ff.*]

1159 KNACHEL, Phillip A., Ed. *Eikon Basilike: The Potraiture of His Sacred Majesty in His Solitudes and Suffering.* Ithaca: Cornell Univ. Press, 1966. [An edition of the work which Milton opposes in *Eikonoklastes.*]

1160 KNIGHTS, L. C. "Hooker and Milton: A Contrast of Styles." *Public Voices: Literature and Politics with Special Reference to the Seventeenth Century.* Totowa, N. J.: Rowman and Littlefield, 1972, pp. 52–70. [He contrasts the "open" political stance of Hooker with the "closed" one of Milton, which "attempts to dominate and control the listener or reader."]

1161 KRANIDAS, Thomas. "Milton and the Rhetoric of Zeal." *TSLL,* 6 (1965), 423–432. [An examination of a Puritan tradition of zeal (based on Revelation 3:16) as a background for understanding the vehement language of Milton's prose.]

1162 LAUDER, William. *King Charles I Vindicated from the Charge of Plagiarism Brought against Him by Milton, and Milton Himself Convicted of Forgery, and a Gross Imposition on the Publick.* London, 1754.

1163 LE COMTE, Edward S. "*Areopagitica* as a Scenario for *Paradise Lost.*" *Achievements of the Left Hand.* Ed. Michael Lieb and John T. Shawcross **(488)**, pp. 121–141.

1164 LEWALSKI, Barbara Kiefer, "Milton: Political Beliefs and Polemical Methods, 1659–60," *PMLA,* 74 (1959), 191–202.

1165 LIEB, Michael. "Milton's *Of Reformation* and the Dynamics of Controversy." *Achievements of the Left Hand.* Ed. Michael Lieb and John T. Shawcross **(488)**, pp. 55–82.

1166 MOHL, Ruth. *John Milton and His Commonplace Book.* New York: Ungar, 1969.

1167 NEUMANN, Joshua H. "Milton's Prose Vocabulary." *PMLA,* 60 (1945), 102–120.

STUDIES OF INDIVIDUAL WORKS

1168 NICHOLAS, Constance, *Introduction and Notes to Milton's History of Britain, Designed To Be Used with Volume X, Columbia Edition, The Works of Milton.* Urbana: Univ. of Illinois Press, 1957.

1169 ONG, Walter J., S. J. "Logic and the Epic Muse: Reflections on Noetic Structures in Milton's Milieu." *Achievements of the Left Hand.* Ed. Michael Lieb and John T. Shawcross (**488**), pp. 239–268.

1170 PARKER, William R. "Milton's Commonplace Book: An Index and Notes." *Milton N,* 3 (1969), 41–54. [Ed. John T. Shawcross.]

1171 PARKS, George B. "Milton's *Moscovia* Not History." *PQ, 31 (1952), 218–221.*

1172 PATRICK, J. Max. "Significant Aspects of the Miltonic State Papers." *HLQ,* 33 (1970), 321–330.

1172A PATTERSON, Annabel. "The Civic Hero in Milton's Prose." *Milton Studies VIII* (1975), 71–101.

1173 POWELL, Chilton L. "The Date and Occasion of Milton's First Divorce Tract." *English Domestic Relations, 1487–1653.* New York: Columbia Univ. Press, 1917, pp. 225–231.

1173A PRICE, Alan F. "Incidental Imagery in *Areopagitica.*" *MP,* 49 (1952), 217–222.

1174 READ, Herbert. "The *Areopagitica.*" *A Coat of Many Colors.* London: Routledge & Kegan Paul, 1945, pp. 333–346.

1175 ROSENBERG, D. M. "Parody of Style in Milton's Polemics." *Milton Studies II* (1970), 113–118.

1176 ROSENBERG, D. M. "Satirical Techniques in Milton's Polemical Prose." *Satire Newsletter,* 8 (1971), 91–97.

1177 SAMUEL, Irene. "Milton and the Ancients on the Writing of History." *Milton Studies II* (1970), 131–148.

1178 SANDLER, FLORENCE. "Icon & Iconoclast." *Achievements of the Left Hand.* Ed. Michael Lieb and John T. Shawcross (**488**), pp. 160–184.

1179 SHAWCROSS, John T. "The Higher Wisdom of *The Tenure of Kings and Magistrates.*" *Achievements of the Left Hand.* Ed. Michael Lieb and John T. Shawcross (**488**), pp. 142–159.

1180 SHAWCROSS, John T. "A Survey of Milton's Prose Works." *Achievements of the Left Hand.* Ed. Michael Lieb and John T. Shawcross (**488**), pp. 292–391.

1181 SIEBERT, F. S. "The Control of the Press During the Puritan Revolution." *Freedom of the Press in England, 1476–1776: The Rise and Decline of Government Controls.* Urbana: Univ. of Illinois Press, 1952, pp. 165–236. [Background for *Areopagitica.*]

1182 SIRLUCK, Ernest. "Milton's Political Thought: The First Cycle." *MP,* 61 (1964), 209–224. [Traces 1649–1654 pattern: Milton began by applying ideas of natural law developed in Divorce Tracts to political theory: then, in justifying the Commonwealth, moved toward providential and theocratic conception of the state, based on the authority of the regenerate minority.]

1182A SMALLENBURG, Harry. "Contiguities and moving Limbs: Style as Argument in *Areopagitica,*" *Milton Studies IX* (1976), 169–184.

1183 SMALLENBERG, Harry. "Government of the Spirit: Style, Structure and Theme In *Treatise of Civil Power.*" *Achievements of the Left Hand.* Ed. Michael Lieb and John T. Shawcross (**488**), pp. 219–238.

73

1184 STAVELY, Keith W. *The Politics of Milton's Prose Style.* New Haven and London: Yale Univ. Press, 1975.

1185 STAVELY, Keith W. "The Style and Structure of Milton's *Readie and Easie Way.*" *Milton Studies V* (1973), 269–287. [Reprinted in **1184.**]

1186 SVENDSEN, Kester. "Milton and Alexander More: New Documents." *JEGP,* 60 (1961), 796–807.

1187 SVENDSEN, Kester. "Milton and the Hundred Articles Against Alexander More." *Th' Upright Heart and Pure.* Ed. Amadeus P. Fiore **(483)**, pp. 117–130.

1188 SVENDSEN, Kester. "Milton's *Pro Se Defensio* and Alexander More." *TSLL,* 1 (1959), 11–29.

1189 SVENDSEN, Kester. "Precepts of Beneficence in Prose." *Milton and Science.* Cambridge: Harvard Univ. Press, 1956, pp. 211–224. [A commentary on the imagery of *The Doctrine and Discipline of Divorce,* and on affinities between the use of figurative elements in the prose and in the poetry.]

1190 TILLYARD, E. M. W. "Private Correspondence and Academic Exercises." *Studies in Milton* **(569)**, pp. 107–136.

1191 VIA, John A. "Milton's Antiprelatical Tracts: The Poet Speaks in Prose." *Milton Studies V* (1973), 87–127. [Thematic and imagistic affinities between the antiprelatical tracts and the early poetry and academic prose.]

1192 WEBBER, Joan. "John Milton: The Prose Style of God's English Poet." *The Eloquent "I": Style and Self in Seventeenth-Century Prose.* Madison, Milwaukee, London: Univ. of Wisconsin Press, 1968, pp. 184–218.

1192A WHITAKER, Juanita. " 'The Wars of Truth': Wisdom and Strength in *Areopagitica,*" *Milton Studies IX* (1976), 185–201.

1193 WHITING, George W. "The Sources of *Eikonoklastes:* A Resurvey." *SP,* 32 (1935), 74–103.

1194 WITTREICH, Joseph Anthony, Jr. " 'The Crown of Eloquence': The Figure of the Orator in Milton's Prose Works." *Achievements of the Left Hand.* Ed. Michael Lieb and John T. Shawcross **(488)**, pp. 3–54.

1195 WITTREICH, Joseph Anthony, Jr. "Milton's *Areopagitica:* Its Isocratic and Ironic Contexts." *Milton Studies IV* (1972), 101–115.

1196 WOOLRYCH, Austin. "Milton & Cromwell: 'A Short but Scandalous Night of Interruption'?" *Achievements of the Left Hand.* Ed. Michael Lieb and John T. Shawcross **(488)**, pp. 185–218.

Special Topics

Text

1197 ADAMS, Robert M. "The Text of *Paradise Lost:* Emphatic and Unemphatic Spellings." *MP,* 52 (1954), 84–91.

1198 DARBISHIRE, Helen, ed. *The Manuscript of* Paradise Lost, *Book* I. Oxford: Oxford Univ. Press, 1931.

1199 DIEKHOFF, John S. "The Text of *Comus,* 1634 to 1645." *PMLA,* 52 (1937), 705–728.

1200 EVANS, G. Blakemore. "The State of Milton's Text: The Prose, 1643–48." *JEGP,* 59 (1960), 497–505.

1201 LOCKWOOD, Laura E. "Milton's Corrections to the *Minor Poems.*" *MLN,* 25 (1910), 201–205.

1202 MACKAIL, John W. "Bentley's Milton." *Studies in Humanism.* London: Longmans, 1938, pp. 186–209. [First appeared in *Proceedings of the British Academy,* 11 (1924), 21ff.]

1203 MADAN, F. F. "Milton, Salmasius and Dugard." *Library,* 4th Ser., 4 (1923), [119]–145. [Reprinted, London: Oxford Univ. Press, 1923. Both printings contain facsimiles.]

1204 PARKER, William Riley. "Above All Liberties: John Milton's Relations with His Earliest Publishers." *Princeton Univ. Library Chronicle,* 2 (1941), 512–515.

1205 PARKER, William Riley. "Milton, Rothwell, and Simmons." *Libr.,* 4th. Ser. 18 (1938), 89–103.

1206 PEARCE, Zachary. *A Review of the Text of the Twelve Books of Milton's* Paradise Lost: *In Which the Chief of Dr. Bentley's Emendations Are Consider'd; and Several Other Emendations and Observations Are Offer'd to the Public.* London: John Shuckburgh, 1733. [First published in three parts in 1732.]

1207 PERSHING, James H. "The Different States of the First Edition of *Paradise Lost.*" *Library,* 4th Ser. 22 (1941), 34–66.

1208 SHAWCROSS, John T. "Establishment of a Text of Milton's Poems Through a Study of *Lycidas.*" PBSA, 56 (1962), 317–331.

1209 SHAWCROSS, John T. "One Aspect of Milton's Spelling: Idle Final 'E.' " *PMLA,* 78 (1963), 501–510.

1210 SHAWCROSS, John T. "Orthography and the Text of *Paradise Lost.*" *Language and Style in Milton.* Ed. Ronald Emma and John T. Shawcross **(482)**, pp. 120–153.

1211 SHAWCROSS, John T. "What We Can Learn from Milton's Spelling." *HLQ,* 26 (1963), 351–361.

1212 TREIP, Mindele. *Milton's Punctuation and Changing English Usage, 1582–1676.* London: Methuen, 1970.

1213 WRIGHT, W. Aldis, ed. *Facsimile of the Manuscript of Milton's Minor Poems Preserved in the Library of Trinity College, Cambridge.* Cambridge: Cambridge Univ. Press, 1899.

Language

1213A CAMPBELL, Gordon. "Milton's *Accedence Commenc't Grammar.*" *Milton Q,* 10 (1976), 39–48.

1214 CLARK, Evert M. "Milton's English Poetical Vocabulary." *SP,* 53 (1956), 220–238.

1215 DARBISHIRE, Helen. "Milton's Poetic Language." *E&S,* 10 (1957), 31–52.

1216 DAVIES, Hugh Sykes. "Milton and the Vocabulary of Verse and Prose." *Literary English Since Shakespeare.* Ed. George Watson. London, Oxford, New York: Oxford Univ. Press, 1970, pp. 175–193. [Galaxy]†

1217 DOBSON, E. J. "Milton's Pronunciation." *Language and Style in Milton.* Ed. Ronald D. Emma and John T. Shawcross **(482)**, pp. 154–192.

1218 EKFELT, Fred Emil. "The Graphic Diction of Milton's English Prose." *PQ,* 25 (1946), 46–69.

1219 EMMA, Ronald D. "Grammar and Milton's English Style." *Language and Style in Milton.* Ed. Ronald D. Emma and John T. Shawcross **(482)**, pp. 233–251.

1220 EMMA, Ronald David. *Milton's Grammar.* The Hague: Mouton, 1964.

1221 HULME, Hilda M. "On the Language of *Paradise Lost:* Its Elizabethan and Early Seventeenth-Century Background." *Language and Style in Milton.* Ed. Ronald D. Emma and John T. Shawcross **(482)**, pp. 65–101.

1222 MILES, Josephine. *The Primary Language of Poetry in the 1640's.* Berkeley: Univ. of California Press, 1948. [Reprinted in part in *The Continuity of Poetic Language.* Berkeley and Los Angeles: Univ. of California Press, 1951.]

1223 SCOTT, F. S. "Some Observations on the Syntax of *Paradise Lost.*" *Australian Universities Language and Literature Association: Proceedings and Papers of the Twelfth Congress Held at the University of Western Australia, 5–11 February 1969.* Ed. A. P. Treweek. Sidney: AULLA, 1970, pp. 211–223.

Prosody

1224 BANKS, Theodore H., Jr. "Miltonic Rhythm: A Study of the Relation of the Full Stops to the Rhythm of *Paradise Lost.*" *PMLA,* 42 (1927), 140–145.

1225 BEUM, Robert. "So Much Gravity and Ease." *Language and Style in Milton.* Ed. Ronald D. Emma and John T. Shawcross **(482)**, pp. 333–368.

1226 BRIDGES, Robert. *Milton's Prosody.* Oxford: Oxford Univ. Press, 1893. [Reprinted, with additional essays and notes by William Johnson Stone, Oxford: Oxford Univ. Press, 1921.]

1227 COOK, Albert S. "Milton's Abstract Music." *UTQ,* 29 (1960), 370–385. [Reprinted in **476.**]

1228 DIEKHOFF, John S. "Milton's Prosody in the Poems of the Trinity Manuscript." *PMLA,* 54 (1939), 153–183.

1229 DIEKHOFF, John S. "Rhyme in *Paradise Lost.*" *PMLA,* 49 (1934), 539–543.

1230 DIEKHOFF, John S. "Terminal Pause in Milton's Verse." *SP,* 32 (1935), 235–239.

1231 EVANS, Robert O. *Milton's Elisions.* Gainesville: Univ. of Florida Press, 1966.

1232 FLETCHER, Harris F. "A Possible Origin of Milton's 'Counterpoint' or Double Rhythm." *JEGP,* 54 (1955), 521–525.

1233 FREEDMAN, Morris. "Milton and Dryden on Rhyme." *HLQ,* 24 (1961), 337–344.

SPECIAL TOPICS

1234 HOLLANDER, John. " 'Sense Variously Drawn Out': On English Enjamb-
ment." *Vision and Resonance: Two Senses of Poetic Form.* New York: Oxford
Univ. Press, 1975, pp. 91–116. [The use of enjambment and variety of pauses in
Milton's blank verse is central to his discussion.]

1235 HUNTER, William B., Jr. "The Sources of Milton's Prosody." *PQ,* 28 (1949),
125–144.

1236 JOHNSON, Lee M. "Milton's Blank Verse Sonnets." *Milton Studies V* (1973),
129–153. [Discovers blank verse units of 14 lines in *PL, PR,* and *SA.*]

1237 KELLOG, George A. "Bridges' *Milton's Prosody* and Renaissance Metrical
Theory." *PMLA,* 68 (1953), 268–285.

1238 LEAVIS, F. R. "Milton's Verse." *Scrutiny,* 2 (1933), 123–136. [Reprinted in
Revaluation: Tradition and Development in English Poetry. London: Chatto &
Windus, 1936 [Norton, 1963]†, and in **492.**]

1239 ORAS, Ants. *Blank Verse and Chronology in Milton.* Gainesville: Univ. of Florida
Press, 1966. [A forty-two-page introduction, followed by thirty-eight pages of
graphs and statistical charts. Cf. **466.**]

1240 ORAS, Ants. "Milton's Blank Verse and the Chronology of His Major Poems."
SAMLA Studies in Milton. Ed. J. Max Patrick. Gainesville: Univ. of Florida Press,
1953, pp. 128–197.

1241 PRINCE F. T. *The Italian Element in Milton's Verse.* Oxford: Clarendon Press,
1954. [Ch. 7, "Milton's Blank Verse: The Diction," is reprinted in **489.**]

1242 SMITH, J. C. "Feminine Endings in Milton's Blank Verse." *TLS,* 5 Dec., 1936,
p. 1016.

1243 SPROTT, S. Ernest. *Milton's Art of Prosody.* Oxford: Blackwell, 1953.

1244 WEISMILLER, Edward R. "Studies of Verse Form in The Minor English Poems." *A Variorum Commentary on the Poems of John Milton.* Ed. Merritt Y.
Hughes. New York: Columbia Univ. Press, 1972. Vol. II, Part Three, pp. 1007–
1087. See also vols. IV and VI of the *Variorum* (16) for further studies of the
prosody by Weismiller.

1245 WHEELER, Thomas. "Milton's Blank Verse Couplets." *JEGP,* 66 (1967), 359–
368. [By "couplets" he means "two-line units, gramatically independent and
linked by their sense and their construction."]

1246 WHITELEY, M. "Verse and Its Feet." *RES,* 9 (1958), 268–279.

Style and Imagery

1247 BANKS, Theodore H. *Milton's Imagery.* New York: Columbia Univ. Press, 1950.

1248 BINYON, Laurence. "A Note on Milton's Imagery and Rhythm." *Seventeenth-
Century Studies Presented to Sir Herbert Grierson.* Oxford: Clarendon Press, 1938,
pp. 184–191.

1249 BROADBENT, J. B. "Milton's Rhetoric." *MP,* 56 (1959), 224–242. [Reprinted
in **496.**]

1249A CAMÉ, Jean-François. "Les Structures fondamentales de l'únivers imaginaire
Miltonien." Clamecy, France: Didier, 1976. [*Études Anglaises* 59]

1250 CHATMAN, Seymour. "Milton's Participial Style." *PMLA,* 83 (1968), 1386–
1399.

SPECIAL TOPICS

1251 CLUTTON-BROCK, A. "Description in Milton." *E&S,* 2 (1911), 99–102.

1252 DANIELLS, Roy. "Baroque Form in English Literature." *UTQ,* 14 (1945), 393–408.

1253 DANIELLS, Roy. *Milton, Mannerism and Baroque.* Toronto: Univ. of Toronto Press, 1963.

1254 ELIOT, T. S. "A Note on the Verse of John Milton." *E&S,* 21 (1936), 32–40. [Reprinted in *T. S. Eliot: Selected Prose.* Ed. John Hayward (Penguin, 1953), in *On Poetry and Poets* (Faber, 1957), and in **489.** This essay and *Milton* (**1556**) were reprinted by Faber under the title *Milton: Two Studies.* [Noonday]†

1254A FRYE, Roland M. "Milton's *Paradise Lost* and the Visual Arts." *PAPS,* 120 (1976), 233–244.

1255 KOEHLER, G. Stanley. "Milton's Use of Color and Light." *Milton Studies III* (1971), 55–81.

1256 LANGDON, Ida. *Milton's Theory of Poetry and Fine Art.* New Haven: Yale Univ. Press, 1924. [Reprinted by Russell, 1965.]

1257 LEAVIS, F. R. "In Defense of Milton." *Scrutiny,* 7 (1938), 104–114. [Reprinted in *The Common Pursuit.* London: Chatto & Windus, 1952, pp. 33–43. (Penguin, 1962.)†]

1258 LEAVIS, F. R. "Mr. Eliot and Milton." *Sewanee Review,* 57 (1949), 1–30. [Reprinted in *The Common Pursuit* (1257), pp. 9–32.]

1259 LERNER, L. D. "The Miltonic Simile." *Essays in Criticism,* 4 (1954), 297–308.

1260 MACKIN, Cooper R. "Aural Imagery as Miltonic Metaphor." *Explorations of Literature.* Ed. Rima Drell Reck. Baton Rouge: Louisiana State Univ. Press, 1966, pp. 32–42.

1261 MAHOOD, M. M. "Milton: The Baroque Artist." *Poetry and Humanism* (544), pp. 169–206.

1262 MAJOR, John M. "Milton's View of Rhetoric." *SP,* 64 (1967), 685–711.

1262A MILLER, George E. "Stylistic Rhetoric and the Language of God in *Paradise Lost,* Book III." *Language and Style,* 8 (1975), 111–126.

1262B MURRIN, Michael. "The Language of Milton's Heaven." *MP,* 74 (1977), 350–365.

1262C NORFORD, Don Parry. "The Sacred Head: Milton's Solar Mysticism." *Milton Studies IX* (1976), 37–75. [Imagery]

1262D RAJAN, Balachandra. "The Cunning Resemblance." *Milton Studies VII* (1975), 29–48.

1263 RICKS, Christopher. *Milton's Grand Style* (**937**). [Pages 78–102 of Ch. 3 are reprinted, with slight changes, in **492.**]

1264 RIX, Herbert David. *Rhetoric in Spenser's Poetry.* State College: Pennsylvania State College [1940]. [Includes discussion of Renaissance rhetorical figures which Milton inherited.]

1265 ROSS, Malcolm M. "Milton and the Protestant Aesthetic." *Poetry and Dogma* (**943**), pp. 183–204.

1266 SAMUEL, Irene. "Milton on Style." *Cornell Library Journal,* 9 (1969), 39–58.

1267 SCOTT, William O. "Ramism and Milton's Concept of Poetic Fancy." *PQ,* 42 (1963), 183–189.

1268 SHUMAKER, Wayne. *Unpremeditated Verse: Feeling and Perception in Paradise Lost* (**954**). [See Chapters 3 through 9.]

1268A SMITH, George William, Jr. "Iterative Rhetoric in *Paradise Lost.*" *MP,* 74 (1976), 1–19.

1269 STEADMAN, John M. "Milton's Rhetoric: Satan and the 'Unjust Discourse.'." *Milton Studies I* (1969), 67–92.

1270 TUVE, Rosemond. "Baroque and Mannerist Milton?" *JEGP,* 60 (1961), 817–833. [Reprinted in **570.**]

1271 TUVE, Rosemond. *Elizabethan and Metaphysical Imagery: Renaissance Poetic and Twentieth-Century Critics.* Chicago: Univ. of Chicago Press, 1947. [Phoenix, 1961.]†

1272 TUVE, Rosemond. *Images and Themes in Five Poems by Milton* (**570A**). ["L'Allegro" and "Il Penseroso," Nativity Ode, "Lycidas," *Comus.*]

1273 WATKINS, W. B. C. "Sensation." *An Anatomy of Milton's Verse* (**573**), pp. 3–41.

1274 WEAVER, Richard M. "Milton's Heroic Prose." *The Ethics of Rhetoric.* Chicago: Regnery, 1953, pp. 143–163. [Reprinted, 1963.]

1275 WHALER, James. "Animal Simile in *Paradise Lost.*" *PMLA,* 47 (1932), 534–553.

1276 WHALER, James. "Compounding and Distribution of Similes in *Paradise Lost.*" *MP,* 28 (1931), 313–327.

1277 WHALER, James. *Counterpoint and Symbol. An Inquiry into the Rhythm of Milton's Epic Style.* Copenhagen: Rosenkilde & Bagger, 1956.

1278 WHALER, James. "The Miltonic Simile." *PMLA,* 46 (1931), 1034–1074.

1279 WIDMER, Kingsley. "The Iconography of Renunciation: The Miltonic Simile." *ELH,* 25 (1958), 258–269. [Reprinted in **479** and, in revised form, in **492.**]

1280 WILDING, Michael. "Milton's Critics: Another Ten Years." *Melbourne Critical Review,* no. 7 (1964), 126–135. [Reviews recent attempts to counter objections to Milton's style through close reading.]

Sources, Analogues, and Comparative Studies

1281 AGAR, Herbert. *Milton and Plato.* Princeton: Princeton Univ. Press, 1928. [Reprinted, Oxford: Oxford Univ. Press, 1931.]

1282 ANDREINI, Giambattista. *L'Adamo.* Ed. Ettore Allodoli. Lanciano: Carabba, 1913.

1283 ARTHOS, John. *Dante, Michelangelo, and Milton.* London: Routledge & Kegan Paul, 1963; New York: Humanities Press, 1964. [The chapter on Milton (pp. 90–120) shows how the poet's theories and achievements, in comparison with those of Michelangelo and Dante, bear out Longinus' principles of elevation in literature.]

1284 BAILEY, M. L. *Milton and Jakob Boehme: a Study of German Mysticism in Seventeenth-Century England.* New York: Oxford Univ. Press, 1914.

SPECIAL TOPICS

1285 BALDWIN, Edward C. "Milton and Phineas Fletcher." *JEGP,* 33 (1934), 544–546.

1286 BALDWIN, Edward C. "Some Extra-Biblical Semitic Influences upon Milton's Story of the Fall of Man." *JEGP,* 28, (1929), 366–401.

1287 BRINKLEY, Roberta F. "Milton and the Arthurian Story." *Arthurian Legend in the Seventeenth Century.* Baltimore: Johns Hopkins Univ. Press, 1932, pp. 126–141. [Reprinted by Octagon Books, 1967.]

1288 BROADBENT, J. B. "Milton's Hell." *ELH,* 21 (1954), 161–192. [Geography and literary background.]

1289 BRODWIN, Leonora Leet. "Milton and the Renaissance Circe." *Milton Studies VI* (1975), 21–83.

1290 BULLOUGH, Geoffrey. "Milton and Cats." *Essays in English Literature from the Renaissance to the Victorian Age Presented to A. S. P. Woodhouse.* Ed. Millar Maclure and F. W. Watt. Toronto: Univ. of Toronto Press, 1964, pp. 103–124. [Milton's possible knowledge of the Dutch poet's treatment of Adam and Eve in "The Marriage Ring" (1637); with translations of analogous passages.]

1291 BUSH, Douglas. *Classical Influences in Renaissance Literature.* Cambridge: Harvard Univ. Press, 1952.

1292 BUSH, Douglas. *Mythology and the Renaissance Tradition in English Poetry.* Minneapolis: Univ. of Minnesota Press; London: Oxford Univ. Press, 1932. [Norton, 1963]† [Reprinted, New York: Pageant Book Co., 1957. A chapter on Milton, pp. 248–286.]

1293 BUXTON, John. "A Note on *Paradise Lost,* x. 71–79." *RES,* 15 (1964), 52–53. [Explained by a passage in Tasso.]

1294 CAWLEY, Robert R. *Milton and the Literature of Travel.* Princeton: Princeton Univ. Press, 1951.

1295 CORCORAN, Sister Mary Irma. *Milton's Paradise with Reference to the Hexameral Background.* Washington: Catholic Univ. of America Press, 1945.

1296 CORY, Herbert E. *Spenser, the School of the Fletchers, and Milton.* Berkeley: Univ. of California Press, 1912.

1296A CURRAN, Stuart. "The Siege of Hateful Contraries: Shelley, Mary Shelley, Byron and *Paradise Lost.*" *Milton and the Line of Vision.* Ed. Joseph Antony Wittreich, Jr. **(500A),** pp. 209–230.

1296B DI SALVO, Jackie. "Blake Encountering Milton: Politics and the Family in *Paradise Lost* and *The Four Zoas.*" *Milton and the Line of Vision.* Ed. Joseph Antony Wittreich, Jr. **(500A),** pp. 143–184.

1297 DOUGLAS, John. *Milton Vindicated from the Charge of Plagiarism Brought against Him by Mr. Lauder, and Lauder Himself Convicted of Several Forgeries and Gross Impositions on the Publick.* London, 1751.

1298 DUNSTER, Charles. *Considerations on Milton's Early Reading and the Prima Stamina of His Paradise Lost; together with Extracts from a Poet of the Sixteenth Century* [Du Bartas, in Sylvester's translation]. *In a Letter to William Falconer, M.D., from Charles Dunster.* London: John Nichols, 1800.

1299 EDMUNDSON, George. *Milton and Vondel.* London: Trübner, 1885.

1300 EVANS, John Martin. *Paradise Lost and the Genesis Tradition.* Oxford: Clarendon Press, 1968.

1301 FERRY, Anne D. *Milton and the Miltonic Dryden.* Cambridge. Harvard Univ. Press, 1968.

1302 FISCH, Harold. "Hebraic Style and Motifs in *Paradise Lost.*" *Language and Style in Milton.* Ed. Ronald D. Emma and John T. Shawcross **(482)**, pp. 30–64.

1303 FLETCHER, Harris F. *Milton's Rabbinical Readings.* Urbana: Univ. of Illinois Press, 1930. [Reprinted by Gordian. See **1359.**]

1304 FLETCHER, Harris F. *Milton's Semitic Studies and Some Manifestations of Them in His Poetry.* Chicago: Univ. of Chicago Press, 1926. [Reprinted by Gordian. See **1359.**]

1305 GIAMATTI, A. Bartlett. *The Earthly Paradise and the Renaissance Epic.* Princeton. Princeton Univ. Press, 1966. [Princeton, 1969]† [Ch. 6 is on Milton.]

1306 GILBERT, Allan H. "Milton and the Mysteries." *SP,* 17 (1920), 147–169.

1307 GILBERT, Allan H. "Milton's Textbook of Astronomy." *PMLA,* 38 (1923), 297–307.

1308 GILBERT, Allan H. "Pierre Davity: His 'Geography' and Its Use by Milton." *Geographical Review,* 7 (1919), 322.

1309 GRANSDEN, K. W. "*Paradise Lost* and The *Aeneid.*" *EIC,* 17 (1967), 281–303.

1310 GREENLAW, Edwin. "A Better Teacher than Aquinas." *SP,* 14 (1917), 196–217. [Spenser.]

1311 GREENLAW, Edwin. "Spenser's Influence on *Paradise Lost.*" *SP,* 17 (1920), 320–359.

1312 GRIERSON, Herbert J. C. *Milton and Wordsworth: Poets and Prophets. A Study of Their Reaction to Political Events.* Cambridge: Cambridge Univ. Press; New York: Macmillan, 1937. [Ch. 6 is reprinted in **499.**]

1313 *The* Adamus Exul *of Grotius, or the Prototype of* Paradise Lost. *Now First Translated from the Latin, by Francis Barham.* London: Sherwood, Gilbert & Piper, 1839.

1314 GURTEEN, S. H. *The Epic of the Fall of Man. A Comparative Study of Caedmon, Dante, and Milton.* New York: Putnam, 1896.

1315 HALKETT, John. *John Milton and the Idea of Matrimony: A Study of the Divorce Tracts and Paradise Lost.* New Haven: Yale Univ. Press, 1970.

1316 HALLER, William. "Hail Wedded Love." *ELH,* 13 (1946), 79–97. [Background for Milton's ideas on marriage and divorce. Reprinted in **496.**]

1317 HANFORD, James Holly. "That Shepherd Who First Taught the Chosen Seed: A Note on Milton's Mosaic Inspiration." *UTQ,* 8 (1939), 403–419.

1318 HARDING, Davis P. *The Club of Hercules: Studies in the Classical Background of Paradise Lost.* Urbana: Univ. of Illinois Press, 1962.

1319 HARDING, Davis P. *Milton and the Renaissance Ovid.* Urbana: Univ. of Illinois Press, 1946.

1320 HARTWELL, Kathleen. *Lactantius and Milton.* Cambridge: Harvard Univ. Press, 1929.

1321 HAZLITT, William. "On Shakespeare and Milton." *Lectures on the English Poets.* London: Taylor & Hessey, 1818. [Partially reprinted in **499.**]

1321A HENNIGER, S. K., Jr. "Sidney and Milton: The Poet as Maker." *Milton and the Line of Vision.* Ed. Joseph Antony Wittreich, Jr. **(500A)**, pp. 57–95.

SPECIAL TOPICS

1322 HERFORD, C. H. *Dante and Milton.* Manchester: Manchester Univ. Press, 1924. [Reprinted in *The Post-War Mind of Germany and Other European Studies.* Oxford: Clarendon Press, 1927, pp. 58–114.]

1322A HIEATT, A. Kent. "Spenser and Milton." *Chaucer Spenser, Milton: Mythopoeic Continuities and Transformations.* Montreal and London: McGill-Queen's Univ. Press, 1975, pp. 153–270.

1322B HOWARD, Donald R. "Flying Through Space: Chaucer and Milton." *Milton and the Line of Vision.* Ed. Joseph Antony Wittreich, Jr. **(500A)**, pp. 3–23.

1323 KIRKCONNELL, Watson. *Awake and the Courteous Echo: The Themes and Prosody of Comus, Lycidas, and Paradise Regained in World Literature with Translations of the Major Analogues.* Toronto: Univ. of Toronto Press, 1973. [Three Appendices: "On Metre," "Biblical Epics," and "Thomas Ellwood's Epic."]

1324 KIRKCONNELL, Watson. *The Celestial Cycle: the Theme of Paradise Lost in World Literature, with Translations of the Major Analogues.* Toronto: Univ. of Toronto Press, 1952. [Reprinted by Gordian.]

1325 KIRKCONNELL, Watson. *That Invincible Samson: The Theme of Samson Agonistes in World Literature, with Translations of the Major Analogues.* Toronto: Univ. of Toronto Press, 1964.

1326 KURTH, Burton O. *Milton and Christian Heroism: Biblical Epic Themes and Forms in Seventeenth-Century England.* Berkeley and Los Angeles: Univ. of California Press, 1959. [Reprinted by Archon, 1966.]

1327 LAUDER, William. *An Essay on Milton's Use and Imitation of the Moderns, in His* Paradise Lost. London: J. Payne & J. Bouquet, 1750. [With a preface by Dr. Johnson.]

1328 LEWALSKI, Barbara Kiefer. "On looking into Pope's Milton." *Études Anglaises,* 27 (1974), 481–500. [A comparative study, using Pope as a "lens" for viewing Milton.]

1329 LOREDANO, Giovanni Francesco. *The Life of Adam.* Ed. Roy C. Flannagan with John Arthos. Gainesville, Florida: Scholars' Facsimiles and Reprints, 1967.

1330 MCCOLLEY, Grant. "The Book of Enoch and *Paradise Lost.*" *HTR,* 31 (1938), 21–39.

1331 MCCOLLEY, Grant. "Milton's Dialogue on Astronomy: The Principal Immediate Sources." *PMLA,* 52 (1937), 728–762.

1332 MCCOLLEY, Grant. Paradise Lost: *An Account of Its Growth and Major Origins, with a Discussion of Milton's Use of Sources and Literary Patterns.* Chicago: Packard, 1940. [Reprinted by Russell, 1963.]

1333 MASSON, David. "The Three Devils: Luther's, Milton's, and Goethe's." *Fraser's Magazine,* 30 (1844), 648–666.

1334 MILLER, Leo. *John Milton Among the Polygamophiles.* New York: Lowenthal Press, 1974.

1335 MOORE, Olin H. "The Infernal Council." *MP,* 16 (1918), 186–193. [Source study.]

1336 MUELLER, Martin E. "Sixteenth-Century Italian Criticism and Milton's Theory of Catharsis." *SEL,* 6 (1966), 139–150.

1337 MUTSCHMANN, Heinrich. *Studies Concerning the Origin of Paradise Lost.* Dorpat: [C. Mattiesen], 1924.

SPECIAL TOPICS

1338 NICOLSON, Marjorie H. *The Breaking of the Circle: Studies in the Effect of the "New Science" upon Seventeenth-Century Poetry.* Rev. ed. New York: Columbia Univ. Press, 1960. [Columbia, 1962]† [First published, Evanston, Illinois: Northwestern Univ. Press, 1950.]

1339 NICOLSON, Marjorie H. "Milton and the Conjectura Cabbalistica." *PQ,* 6 (1927), 1–18.

1340 NICOLSON, Marjorie H. "Milton and the Telescope." *ELH,* 2 (1935), 1–32. [Reprinted in *Science and Imagination.* Ithaca, N.Y.: Cornell Univ. Press, 1956, pp. 58 ff. Also reprinted in **479.**]

1341 NICOLSON, Marjorie H. "Milton's Hell and the Phlegraean Fields." *UTQ,* 7 (1938), 500–513.

1341A NORFORD, Don Parry. "The Sacred Head: Milton's Solar Mysticism." *Milton Studies IX* (1976), 37–75.

1342 RAMSAY, Robert L. "Morality Themes in Milton's Poetry." *SP,* 15 (1918), 123–159.

1343 RAND, E. K. "Milton in Rustication." *SP,* 19 (1922), 109–135. [Milton's study of ancient poets and their influence on him.]

1343A RIEGER, James. "Wordsworth Unalarm'd." *Milton and the Line of Vision.* Ed. Joseph Antony Wittreich, Jr. **(500A),** pp. 185–208.

1344 ROBBINS, F. E. *The Hexaemeral Literature: A Study of the Greek and Latin Commentaries on Genesis.* Chicago: Univ. of Chicago Press, [1912].

1345 SAMUEL, Irene. *Dante and Milton: The Commedia and Paradise Lost.* Ithaca, N.Y.: Cornell Univ. Press, 1966.

1346 SAMUEL, Irene. *Plato and Milton.* Ithaca, N.Y.: Cornell Univ. Press, 1947. [Cornell, 1965]†

1347 SAMUEL, Irene. "The Valley of Serpents: *Inferno* xxiv–xxv and *Paradise Lost* X.504–577." *PMLA,* 78 (1963), 449–451.

1348 SELLIN, Paul R. "Milton and Heinsius: Theoretical Homogeneity." *Medieval Epic to the "Epic Theater" of Brecht.* Ed. Rosario P. Armato and John M. Spalek. Los Angeles: Univ. of Southern California Press, 1968, pp. 125–134.

1349 SIMS, James H. *The Bible in Milton's Epics.* Gainesville, Florida: Univ. of Florida Press, 1962.

1350 SIMS, James H. "Camoen's 'Lusiads' and Milton's 'Paradise Lost': Satan's Voyage to Eden." *Papers on Milton.* Ed. Philip M. Griffith and Lester F. Zimmerman **(484),** pp. 36–46.

1351 SPAETH, Sigmund G. *Milton's Knowledge of Music: Its Sources and Its Significance in His Works.* Princeton: Princeton Univ. Library, 1913. [Ann Arbor, 1963]† [Includes bibliography of sources of musical theory.]

1352 STARNES, D. T., and TALBERT, Ernest W. "Milton and the Dictionaries." *Classical Myth and Legend in Renaissance Dictionaries: A Study of Renaissance Dictionaries in Their Relation to the Classical Learning of Contemporary English Writers.* Chapel Hill: Univ. of North Carolina Press, 1955, pp. 226–239.

1353 STEADMAN, John M. "Chaste Muse and 'Casta Juventus': Milton, Minturno, and Scaliger on Inspiration and the Poet's Character." *Italica,* 40 (1963), 28–34.

SPECIAL TOPICS

1354 STEADMAN, John M. "Milton and Renaissance Epic Theory." *Medieval Epic to the "Epic Theater" of Brecht.* Ed. Rosario P. Armato and John M. Spalek. Los Angeles: Univ. of Southern California Press, 1968, pp. 109–124. [Partially reprinted in **962A.**]

1355 STEADMAN, John M. *Milton and the Renaissance Hero.* Oxford: Clarendon Press, 1967.

1356 STEADMAN, John M. *Milton's Epic Characters: Image and Idol.* Chapel Hill: Univ. of North Carolina Press, 1968.

1357 STEADMAN, John M. "The Tragic Glass: Milton, Minturno, and The *Condition Humaine.*" *Th' Upright Heart and Pure.* Ed. Amadeus P. Fiore (**483**), pp. 101–115. [The theme of the misery (and dignity) of the human condition in *PL* and *SA.*]

1358 STEADMAN, John M. "Urania, Wisdom, and Scriptural Exegesis (*Paradise Lost,* VII. 1–12)." *Neophilologus,* 47 (1963), 61–73.

1359 STOLLMAN, Samuel S. "Milton's Rabbinical Readings and Fletcher." *Milton Studies IV* (1972), 195–215.

1360 STROUP, Thomas B. *Religious Rite & Ceremony in Milton's Poetry.* Lexington: Univ. of Kentucky Press, 1968.

1361 SVENDSEN, Kester. *Milton and Science.* Cambridge: Harvard Univ. Press, 1956. [Reprinted by Greenwood Press, 1969. Comprehensive study of natural science in Milton based on the Medieval and Renaissance encyclopedias and other sources of popular learning current in his time.]

1362 TATLOCK, John S. P. "Milton's Sin and Death." *MLN,* 21 (1906), 239–240. [Variety of sources for figures of Sin and Death in *Paradise Lost.*]

1363 TAYLOR, George C. *Milton's Use of Du Bartas.* Cambridge: Harvard Univ. Press; London: Milford, 1934. [Reprinted by Octagon Books, 1967.]

1364 TAYLOR, George C. "Shakspere and Milton Again." *SP,* 23 (1926), 189–199.

1365 THALER, Alwin. "Shakespearean Recollections in Milton: A Summing Up." *Shakespeare and Our World.* Knoxville: Univ. of Tennessee Press, 1966, pp. 139–227.

1366 THALER, Alwin. "The Shaksperian Element in Milton." *PMLA,* 40 (1925), 645–691. [Reprinted in *Shakspere's Silences.* Cambridge: Harvard Univ. Press, 1929, 139–208.]

1367 THOMPSON, Elbert N. S. "Milton's Knowledge of Geography." *SP,* 16 (1919), 148–171.

1368 TILLYARD, E. M. W. *The Metaphysicals and Milton.* London: Chatto & Windus, 1956.

1369 TILLYARD, E. M. W. "Milton and Longinus." *TLS,* Aug. 28, 1930, p. 684.

1370 VALVASONE, Erasmo di. *L'Angeleida, poema ... per servire d'appendice al Paradiso perduto di Milton trad. da Polidori.* London, 1842.

1370A WEBBER, Joan. "Walking on Water: Milton, Stevens and Contemporary Poetry." *Milton and the Line of Vision.* Ed. Joseph Antony Wittreich, Jr. (**500A**), pp. 231–268.

1371 WEISINGER, Herbert. *Tragedy and the Paradox of the Fortunate Fall.* London: Routledge & Kegan Paul, 1953.

84

1372 WEISMILLER, Edward. "Materials Dark and Crude: A Partial Genealogy of Milton's Satan." *HLQ*, 31 (1967), 75–93. [Similarities between *PL* and Tasso's *Jerusalem Delivered* (in the Fairfax translation).]

1373 WHITING, George W. *Milton's Literary Milieu.* Chapel Hill: Univ. of North Carolina Press; London: Oxford Univ. Press, 1939. [Reprinted by Russell, 1964.]

1374 WILLIAMS, Arnold. "Commentaries on Genesis as a Basis for Hexaemeral Material in the Literature of the Late Renaissance." *SP*, 34 (1937), 191–208.

1375 WILLIAMS, Arnold. *The Common Expositor: An Account of the Commentaries on Genesis, 1527–1633.* Chapel Hill: Univ. of North Carolina Press, 1948.

1376 WILLIAMS, Arnold. "Milton and the Book of Enoch—An Alternative Hypothesis." *HTR*, 33 (1940), 291–299.

1377 WILLIAMS, Arnold. "Milton and the Renaissance Commentaries on *Genesis*." *MP*, 37 (1940), 263–278.

1377A WILLIAMS, Kathleen. "Milton, Greatest Spenserian." *Milton and the Line of Vision* Ed. Joseph Antony Wittreich, Jr. **(500A)**, pp. 25–55.

1378 WOODHULL, Mariana. *The Epic of* Paradise Lost. New York: Putnam, 1907. [Contains summaries of earlier treatments.]

1379 WÜLCKER, R. "Caedmon und Milton." *Anglia*, 4 (1881), 401–405.

Cosmology

1380 CHAMBERS, A. B. "Chaos in *Paradise Lost.*" *JHI*, 24 (1963), 55–84.

1381 COPE, Jackson I. "Time and Space as Miltonic Symbol." *ELH*, 26 (1959), 497–513.

1382 CURRY, Walter C. "The Genesis of Milton's World." *Anglia*, 70 (1951), 129–149. [Reprinted in **1384.**]

1383 CURRY, Walter C. "Milton's Chaos and Old Night." *JEGP*, 46 (1947), 38–52. [Reprinted in **1384.**]

1384 CURRY, Walter C. *Milton's Ontology, Cosmology, and Physics.* Lexington: Univ. of Kentucky Press, 1957. [Kentucky, 1966]† [Revision of and additions to Curry's earlier studies of Milton's system and its sources.]

1385 GILBERT, Allan H. "The Outside Shell of Milton's World." *SP*, 20 (1923), 444–447.

1386 JOHNSON, Francis Rarick. *Astronomical Thought in Renaissance England: A Study of the English Scientific Writings from 1500 to 1645.* Baltimore: Johns Hopkins Press, 1937.

1387 LOVEJOY, Arthur O. "Milton's Dialogue on Astronomy." *Reason and the Imagination: Studies in the History of Ideas, 1600–1800.* Ed. J. A. Mazzeo. New York: Columbia Univ. Press; London: Routledge & Kegan Paul, 1962, pp. 129–142.

1388 MCCOLLEY, Grant. "The Astronomy of *Paradise Lost.*" *SP*, 34 (1937), 209–247.

1389 ORCHARD, Thomas N. *Milton's Astronomy: The Astronomy of* Paradise Lost. Rev. ed. London: Longmans, Green, 1913. [First published, 1896.]

1390 ROBINS, Harry F. "That Unnecessary Shell of Milton's World." *Studies in Honor of T. W. Baldwin.* Ed. Don Cameron Allen. Urbana: Univ. of Illinois Press, 1958, pp. 211–219.

1391 WHITING, George W. *Milton and This Pendant World.* Austin: Univ. of Texas Press, 1958. [Reprinted by Octagon Books, 1969.]

Religion and Philosophy

1392 ADAMSON, J. H. "Milton's Arianism." *HTR,* 53 (1960), 269–276.

1393 ALLISON, Alexander W. "A Heterodox Note on Milton's Orthodoxy." *PMASAL,* 48 (1963), 621–628.

1394 BEKKER, Hugo. "The Religio-Philosophical Orientations of Vondel's *Lucifer,* Milton's *Paradise Lost,* and Grotius' *Adamus Exul.*" *Neophilologus,* 44 (1960), 234–244.

1394A BERRY, Boyd. *Process of Speech: Puritan Religious Writing and Paradise Lost.* Baltimore and London: Johns Hopkins Univ. Press, 1976.

1395 BOSWELL, Jackson C. "Milton and Prevenient Grace." *SEL,* 7 (1967), 83–94.

1395A BRODWIN, Leonora Leet. "The Dissolution of Satan in *Paradise Lost:* A Study of Milton's Heretical Eschatology." *Milton Studies VIII* (1975), 165–207.

1395B CAMPBELL, Gordon. "*De Doctrina Christiana:* Its Structural Principles and Its Unfinished State." *Milton Studies IX* (1976), 243–260.

1396 CHANNING, William Ellery. *Remarks on the Character and Writings of John Milton; Occasioned by the Publication of His Lately Discovered* Treatise on Christian Doctrine. Boston: Butts, 1896. [First published, *Christian Examiner,* 1826.]

1397 CHAUVET, Paul. *La religion de Milton.* Paris: Didier, 1909.

1398 CLAIR, John A. "A Note on Milton's 'Arianism.' " *Essays and Studies in Language and Literature.* Ed. Herbert H. Petit. Louvain, Belgium: E. Nauwelaerts (Duquesne Univ. Press), 1964, pp. 44–48. [*PL,* III. 305–307 is compatible with Arianism when seen as the culmination of the progressive elevation of the Son.]

1399 CLARK, Ira. "Milton and the Image of God." *JEGP,* 68 (1969), 422–431. [Adam, Eve, and the Son as images of God.]

1399A CLARK, Mili N. "The Mechanics of Creation: Non-contradiction and Natural Necessity in *Paradise Lost.* ELR,* 7 (1977), 207–242.

1400 CONKLIN, George N. *Biblical Criticism and Heresy in Milton.* New York: King's Crown Press, 1949. [Reprinted by Octagon Books, 1972.]

1401 EMPSON, William. *Milton's God.* London: Chatto & Windus, 1961; Norfolk, Conn.: New Directions, 1962. Rev. ed. London: Chatto & Windus, 1965. [An all-out attack on the God of Moses and the God of traditional Christian theology. Milton avoids dwelling on the worst refinements of the latter, and in making God abdicate Satanic tyranny (III, 340 ff.), makes him morally and politically "just tolerable." Milton is a good advocate who anticipates opponents' arguments. He makes the case for Satan, Adam, Eve, and does not mind driving home God's injustice in the process. This is what makes the poem so dramatic and "an echoing chamber for the whole mind of the period." Part of Ch. 4 is reprinted in **492.**]

1401A FIORE, Peter A., O. F. M. " 'Account Mee Man': The Incarnation in *Paradise Lost.* " *HLQ,* 39 (1975), 51–56.

1402 FIXLER, Michael. *Milton and the Kingdoms of God.* Evanston: Northwestern Univ. Press; London: Faber & Faber, 1964. [A reading of Milton against the background of the Apocalyptic tradition and the politico-religious setting, with a long concluding chapter on *PR.*]

1403 FRYE, Roland M. *God, Man, and Satan: Patterns of Christian Thought and Life in* Paradise Lost, Pilgrim's Progress, *and the Great Theologians.* Princeton: Princeton Univ. Press, 1960.

1404 GILBERT, Allan H. "The Theological Basis of Satan's Rebellion and the Function of Abdiel in *Paradise Lost.*" *MP,* 40 (1942), 19–42.

1405 GOHN, Ernest S. "The Christian Ethic of *Paradise Lost* and *Samson Agonistes.*" *SN,* 24 (1962), 243–268.

1406 GRACE, William J. "Milton, Salmasius, and the Natural Law." *JHI,* 24 (1963), 323–336.

1407 HALLER, William. "Milton and the Protestant Ethic." *Journal of British Studies,* no. 1 (1961), pp. 52–57.

1407A HAMLET, Desmond M. *One Greater Man: Justice and Damnation in Paradise Lost.* Lewisburg, Pa.: Bucknell Univ. Press; London: Associated University Presses, 1976.

1408 HENRY, Nathaniel H. "John Milton, Anglican." *Renaissance Papers 1969,* (1970), pp. 57–66.

1409 HUNTER, William B., Jr. "The Heresies of Satan." *Th' Upright Heart and Pure.* Ed. Amadeus P. Fiore (483), pp. 25–34.

1410 HUNTER, William B., Jr. "Milton on the Incarnation: Some More Heresies." *JHI,* 21 (1960), 349–369.

1411 HUNTER, William B., Jr. "Milton's Arianism Reconsidered." *HTR,* 52 (1959), 9–35.

1412 HUNTER, William B., Jr. "Some Problems in John Milton's Theological Vocabulary." *HTR,* 57 (1964), 353–365. [Milton's careful distinction between "substance" and "essence" shows him to be consistent with the Nicene Creed regarding the Trinity.]

1413 HUNTER, William B., PATRIDES, C. A., and ADAMSON, J. H. *Bright Essence: Studies in Milton's Theology.* Salt Lake City: Univ. of Utah Press, 1971. [See **1415, 1417,** and **1422.**]

1414 KASTOR, Frank S. *Milton and the Literary Satan.* Amsterdam: Rodopi, 1974. [A study of the Satan tradition as a background for understanding Milton's depiction of Satan.]

1415 KELLEY, Maurice W. "Milton and the Trinity." *HLQ,* 33 (1970), 315–320. [See **1413** and **1422.**]

1416 KELLEY, Maurice W. "Milton's Arianism Again Considered." *HTR,* 54 (1961), 195–205.

1417 KELLEY, Maurice W. *This Great Argument: a Study of Milton's* De doctrina christiana *as a Gloss upon* Paradise Lost. Princeton: Princeton Univ. Press; Oxford Univ. Press, 1941.

1417A KERRIGAN, William. "The Heritical Milton: From Assumption to Mortalism." *ELR,* 5 (1975), 125–166.

1418 LARSON, Martin A. "Milton and Servetus: a Study in the Sources of Milton's Theology." *PMLA,* 41 (1926), 891–934.

SPECIAL TOPICS

1419 LARSON, Martin A. "Milton's Essential Relationship to Puritanism and Stoicism." *PQ,* 5 (1927), 201–220.

1419A LIEB, Michael. "Paradise Lost and the Myth of Prohibition." *Milton Studies VII* (1975), 233–265.

1420 LOVEJOY, Arthur O. "Milton and the Paradox of the Fortunate Fall." *ELH,* 4 (1937), 161–179. [See **883.**]

1421 MACCALLUM, Hugh R. "Milton and the Figurative Interpretation of the Bible." *UTQ,* 31 (1962), 397–415.

1422 MACCALLUM, Hugh R. " 'Most Perfect Hero': The Role of the Son in Milton's Theodicy." *Paradise Lost: A Tercentenary Tribute.* Ed. Balachandra Rajan **(494),** pp. 79–105. [See **1413** and **1415.**]

1423 MADSEN, William G. *From Shadowy Types to Truth: Studies in Milton's Symbolism.* New Haven: Yale Univ. Press, 1968. [An analysis of Milton's major poems in relation to theories of Biblical interpretation.]

1424 MADSEN, William G. "The Idea of Nature in Milton's Poetry." *Three Studies in the Renaissance: Sydney, Jonson, Milton.* By Richard B. Young, W. Todd Furniss, and William G. Madsen. New Haven: Yale Univ. Press, 1958, pp. 181–283.

1425 MULDROW, George M. *Milton and the Drama of the Soul: A Study of the Theme of Restoration of Men in Milton's Later Poetry.* The Hague: Mouton, 1970. [A. ch. on *CD,* followed by chs. on *PL, PR,* and *SA.*]

1426 NICOLSON, Marjorie H. "Milton and Hobbes." *SP,* 23 (1926), 405–433.

1427 NICOLSON, Marjorie H. "The Spirit World of Milton and More." *SP,* 22 (1925), 433–452. [I.e., Henry More, the Cambridge Platonist.]

1428 PARISH, John E. "Milton and an Anthropomorphic God." *SP,* 56 (1959), 619–625.

1429 PATRIDES, C. A. "Adam's 'Happy Fault' and XVIIth Century Apologetics." *Franciscan Studies,* 23 (1963), 238–243. [Accounts of the paradox of the Fortunate Fall added to those found in 1420.]

1430 PATRIDES, C. A. *The Grand Design of God: The Literary Form of the Christian View of History* **(144).**

1431 PATRIDES, C. A. "Milton and Arianism." *JHI,* 25 (1964), 423–429. [Milton disagrees with eight basic Arian tenets.]

1431A PATRIDES, C. A. "Milton and the Arian Controversy. *PAPS,* 120 (1976), 245–252. [Finds a contrasting treatment of the Son in *PL* and in *De doctrina.*]

1432 PATRIDES, C. A. *Milton and the Christian Tradition.* Oxford: Clarendon Press, 1966. [The most extensive overall treatment of Milton's use of Christian materials.]

1433 PATRIDES, C. A. "Milton and the Protestant Theory of the Atonement." *PMLA,* 74 (1959), 7–13.

1434 PATRIDES, C. A. *"Paradise Lost* and the Language of Theology." *Language and Style in Milton.* Ed. Ronald D. Emma and John T. Shawcross **(482),** pp. 102–119.

1435 PATRIDES, C. A. *The Phoenix and the Ladder: The Rise and Decline of the Christian View of History* **(145).**

1436 PATRIDES, C. A. "Renaissance and Modern Views'on Hell." *HTR,* 57 (1964), 217–236. [The tradition of regarding Hell "both as a condition and as a place," and Milton's place in the tradition.]

1437 PATRIDES, C. A. "The Salvation of Satan." *JHI,* 28 (1967), 467–478.

1438 ROBINS, Harry F. *If This Be Heresy: A Study of Milton and Origen.* Urbana: Univ. of Ill. Press, 1963.

1439 RUPP, Ernest Gordon. "John Milton and 'Paradise Lost'." *Six Makers of English Religion, 1500–1700.* London: Hodder & Stoughton; New York: Harper, 1957.

1440 SEWELL, Arthur. *A Study in Milton's Christian Doctrine.* London: Oxford Univ. Press; London: Milford, 1939. [Reprinted by Shoestring Press, 1967.]

1441 SIMS, James H. *"Paradise Lost:* 'Arian Document' or Christian Poem?" *EA,* 20 (1968), 337–347. [Contains a concise summary of the controversy over Milton's Arianism.]

1442 STAPLETON, Laurence. "Milton's Conception of Time in *The Christian Doctrine." HTR,* 57 (1964), 9–21. [Time existed before the creation of the universe.]

1443 STARKMAN, M. K. "The Militant Miltonist; or, The Retreat from Humanism." *ELH,* 26 (1959), 209–228.

1444 STEADMAN, John M. " 'Man's First Disobedience': The Causal Structure of the Fall." *JHI,* 21 (1960), 180–197. [Reprinted in **564.**]

1445 TAYLOR,. Dick, Jr. "Grace as a Means of Poetry: Milton's Pattern for Salvation." *Tulane Studies in English,* 4 (1954), 57–90.

1446 TAYLOR, Dick, Jr. "Milton and the Paradox of the Fortunate Fall Once More." *TSE,* 9 (1959), 35–51.

1447 TILLYARD, E. M. W. "Theology and Emotion in Milton." *Studies in Milton* (**569**), pp. 137–168.

1448 WEBBER, Joan. "Milton's God." *ELH,* 40 (1973), 514–531.

1449 WEST, Robert H. *Milton and the Angels.* Athens: Univ. of Georgia Press, 1955.

1450 WILLIAMSON, George. "Milton and the Mortalist Heresy." *SP,* 32 (1935), 553–579.

1451 WOODHOUSE, A. S. P. *The Heavenly Muse.* Ed. Hugh MacCallum (**577**). [See Ch. 5, "The theologian, 1: Milton's Christian doctrine," pp. 124–144, and Ch. 6, "The theologian, 2: the creation: the Son of God," pp. 145–175.]

1452 WOODHOUSE, A. S. P. "Milton." *The Poet and His Faith: Religion and Poetry in England from Spenser to Eliot and Auden.* Chicago and London: Univ. of Chicago Press, 1965, pp. 90–122.

1453 WOODHOUSE, A. S. P. "Milton, Puritanism, and Liberty." *UTQ,* 4 (1935), 483–513.

Translations

1454 BAKER, A. T. *Milton and Chateaubriand.* Manchester, 1919.

1455 BARNETT, Pamela R. *Theodore Haak, F.R.S. (1605–1690): The First German Translator of* Paradise Lost. The Hague: Mouton, 1962. [Includes Haak's translation of *PL* I-III.]

1456 BERGE, Ernst Gottlieb, von, trans. *Das Verlustigte Paradeiss.* Zerbst: privately printed, 1682. [Copies much of Haak's translation word for word.]

1457 BERNHARDI, Wilhelm, trans. *John Milton's Politische Haputschriften.* 3 vols. Berlin, 1874, 1876, 1879.

1458 BLONDEL, Jacques, ed. and trans. *John Milton: Le paradis reconquis.* Paris: Aubier, 1955. [A critical introduction, followed by the text of *Paradise Regained* in English and French on facing pages.]

1459 BLONDEL, Jacques. *Le "Comus" de John Milton: masque neptunien.* Paris: Presses universitaires de France, 1964. [Contains a French translation of *Comus* with notes also in French.]

1460 BODMER, Johann Jakob B., trans. *verlohrnes Paradises.* Zurich, 1732. [Reprinted, Zurich, 1769, 1780; Stuttgart, 1965 (facsimile).]

1461 [*Paradise Lost* and *Paradise Regained* translated into Russian prose by] Borodin, Moscow, 1888.

1462 BUYLLA, José Benito A. "La traducción de Jovellanos del libro primero del *Paraiso Perdido,* de Milton." *FMod,* 4, 10 (1963), 1–47. [Includes fully annotated translation.]

1463 CASDAGLI, Alexander S., trans. *Milton's Paradise Lost Now for the First Time Translated into Greek Accentual Dactylic Hexameters. With Illustrations by Gustave Doré.* London: published by translator, 1887.

1464 ČELIDZE, Vahtang, trans. *Poterjannyj raj. Vozvraščennyj raj.* Tbilisi: Sabčota Sakartvelo, 1969. [*Paradise Lost* and *Paradise Regained* in Russian.]

1465 CHATEAUBRIAND, François Auguste René, vicomte de, trans. *Le Paradis perdu de Milton.* 2 vols. Paris: Gosselin & Cie, 1836. [Reprinted in *Édition monument, illustrée par 55 dessins originaux composés par Flatters, gravés au burin sur Acier, par les artistes les plus célèbres de la France et de l'étranger.* Paris [1837]. Reprinted in *précédé de réflexions sur la vie et les écrits de Milton, par Lamartine; et enrichi de vingt-cinq magnifiques estampes originales gravées au burin sur acier.* Paris: Bigot & Voisvenel, 1855.]

1466 DJILAS, Milovan, trans. *Džon Milton: Izqubljeni Raj.* New York: Harcourt, Brace, and World, 1969. [The first Serbo-Croatian translation of *Paradise Lost.*]

1467 DOBSON, William, trans., *Paradisi Amissi Liber primus Graecè, cum celebri versione Latinâ.* Dublin, 1770.

1468 EITNER, Karl, trans. *Das Verlorene Paradies. Episches Gedicht von John Milton.* (Bibliothek Auslandischer Klassiker.) Hildburghausen: Verlag des Bibliographischen Instituts, 1865.

1469 ESCOIQUIZ, Juan, trans. *El Paraiso Perdido.* 3d ed. Barcelona: Editorial Augusta, 1968.

1470 FUSTER, Antonio, trans. *El Paraiso Perdido.* Barcelona: Iberia, 1968.

1471 GRESWELL, E., trans. *Fabulae Samson Agonistes et Comus, Graece.* Oxonii: Excudebat S. Collingwood, veneunt apud J. H. Parker, 1832.

1472 HOG, William, trans. *Paraphrasis Poetica in tria Johannis Miltoni, viri clarissimi, Poemata, viz. Paradisum Amissum, Paradisum Recuperatum, et Samsonem Agonisten.* London: John Darby, 1690.

1473 HSIUNG, Ho Jui, trans. *John Milton: Shih Le Yüan.* Tainan: Kai San Book Store, 1968. [*Paradise Lost* in Chinese.]

1474 JÁNOSY, István, trans. *Elveszett Paradicsom.* Budapest: Magyar Helikon, 1969. [*Paradise Lost* in Hungarian.]

1475 KERVYN, M. G., trans. *Æuvres choisies de Milton.* Paris, 1839. [*Comus,* "L'Allegro," "Il Penseroso," *Samson Agonistes,* "Lycidas," Sonnets, Latin poems.]

1476 KVITAISVILI, E. and Kiknadze, Z., trans. *Samson-Borec.* Tbilisi: Nakaduli, 1966. [*Samson Agonistes* in Georgian.]

1477 LUTAND, O., trans. *Pour la liberté de la presse sans autorisation ni censure.* Paris: Aubier-Flammarion, 1969. [*Areopagitica* in French and English.]

1478 MAGON, Leopold. *Die Drei Ersten Versuche einer Uebersetzungen von Miltons Verlorenern Paradies.* Weimar, 1956.

1479 MARIOTTINI, Felice, trans. *Il Paradiso Perduto di Giovanni Milton, tradotto in verso sciolto italiano.* 3 vols. Rome, 1813–1814. [Mariottini's translation of the first book appeared London, 1794.]

1480 MEIER, Hans Heinrich, trans. *Das verlorene Paradies.* Stuttgart: Reclam, 1969.

1480A MIYANISHI, Mitsuo. *Milton in Japan, 1871–1971.* Tokyo: Kinseido, Ltd., 1975. [Contains an extensive annotated bibliography.]

1481 *PARADISUS Amissa, Poema Heroicum, quod à Joanne Miltono Anglo Anglicè scriptum in decem libros digestum est, nunc autem à viris quibusdam natione eadem oriundis in Linguam Romanam transfertur. Liber Primus.* London: T. Dring, 1686.

1482 POLIDORI, G., trans. *Il Como, favola boschereccia di Giovanni Milton.* Londra: Dulau, 1802.

1483 POLIDORI, G., trans. *Traduzione delle Opere poetiche di Giovanni Milton.* 3 vols. Londra: Stampato presso il traduttore, 1840. [*L'Angeleida* appended to 2d vol. See **1370**.]

1484 RACINE, Louis, trans. *Traduction du Paradis Perdu, chargée de notes.* 3 vols. Paris: Desaint & Saillant, 1755.

1485 RAO, Balakrishna, trans. *Areopagitica.* New Delhi: Sahitya Akademi, 1965. [Hindi.]

1486 RIBERA, J., trans. *El Paraiso Perdido.* Barcelona: Petronio, 1971.

1487 ROBERTS, W. Wright. "Chateaubriand and Milton." *MLR,* 5 (1910), 409–429.

1488 ROSELL, Don Cayetano, trans. *El Paraiso Perdido por John Milton.* Mexico: Union Tipografica Editorial Hispano-Americana 1949. [A translation in Spanish prose, annotated, and preceded by a life of Milton. Also contains a Spanish prose translation of *Paradise Regained* by Enrique Leopoldo de Verneuill.]

1489 SAILLENS, Emile, ed. and trans. *Lycidas et sonnets.* Paris: Aubier-Montaigne, 1971. [Text in English and French.]

1490 ST. MAUR, Nicholas François Dupré de, trans. *Le Paradis Perdu de Milton. Poeme Heroique. Traduit de l'Anglois.* 3 vols. Paris: Cailleau et al., 1729. [Translated into English prose in 1745.]

1491 SANJUAN, Dionisio, trans. *El Paraiso Perdido.* 6th ed. Madrid: Aguilar, 1969.

1492 SCHUHMANN, Bernhard, trans. *Das Verlorene Paradies. Das Wiedergewonnene Paradies.* München: Winkler, 1966.

1493 SIDDIQUI, Zillur Rahman. *Areopagitica.* Dacca: Central Board for Development of Bengali, 1971. [Bengali.]

1494 SILVA, P. José Amaro de, trans. *Paraiso perdido, poëma heroico de J. Milton, traduzido em vulgar. . . . Com o Paraiso restaurado do mesmo author.* 2 vols. Lisbon, 1792.

1495 VAN ZANTEN, J., trans. *'t Paradijs Verlooren: Heldengedicht in Tien Boeken.* Haarlem: Bij Geertruyd van Kessel, 1728. [Dutch blank verse.]

Illustrations, Iconography, and Pictorial Traditions

1496 BAKER, C. H. Collins. "Some Illustrators of Milton's *Paradise Lost* (1688–1850)." *Library,* 5th Ser., 3 (1948–1949), 1–21, 101–119.

1497 BALSTOM, Thomas. "Some Illustrators of Milton's *Paradise Lost.*" *Library,* 5th Ser., 4 (1949), 146–147. [Corrections to **1496.**]

1498 [BARTOLOZZI, F.] *Milton's Paradise Lost. A New Edition. Adorned with Plates Engraved Chiefly by F. Bartolozzi from Designs by W. Hamilton and H. Fuseli.* 2 vols. London: Du Roveray, 1802.

1498A BEHRENDT, Stephen. "Blake's Illustrations to Milton's *Nativity Ode, PQ,* 55 (1976), 65–95.

1498B BEHRENDT, Stephen. "Bright Pilgrimage: William Blake's Designs for *L'Allegro* and *Il Penseroso. Milton Studies VIII* (1975), 123–147.

1499 [BLAKE, William] *L'Allegro: With the Paintings by William Blake, Together with a Note upon the Poem by W. P. Trent.* New York: Limited Editions, 1954.

1500 [BLAKE, William] *Il Penseroso: With the Paintings by William Blake, Together with a Note upon the Poem by Chauncey Brewster Tinker.* New York: Limited Editions, 1954.

1501 [BLAKE, William] *William Blake's Illustrations of Milton's* Comus. *Reproduced by William Griggs.* London, 1890.

1502 [BLAKE, William] *On the Morning of Christ's Nativity. Milton's Hymn with Illustrations by William Blake and a Note by Geoffrey Keynes.* Cambridge: Cambridge Univ. Press, 1923.

1503 [BLAKE, William] *Paradise Lost by John Milton. Illustrations by William Blake.* Liverpool: Lyceum Press, 1906.

1504 [BLAKE, William] Figgis, Darrell. *The Paintings of William Blake.* London: E. Benn, 1925. [Includes all paintings for *PL* and *PR.*]

1505 [BLAKE, William] Baker, C. H. Collins. *An Exhibition of William Blake's Water-Color Drawings of Milton's "Paradise Lost."* San Marino, California: Huntington Library, 1936.

1506 [BLAKE, William] *Paradise Lost. Illustrated by William Blake.* New York: Heritage Press, 1940.

1507 [BLAKE, William] Beeching, Canon, and Geoffrey Keynes, eds. *Poems in English by John Milton, with Illustrations by William Blake.* 2 vols. London: Nonesuch Press, 1926.

1508 [CHERON, Louis] [Illustrations by Cheron and Thornhill for *PL* and *PR* in] *The Poetical Works of Mr. John Milton.* 2 vols. London: J. Tonson, 1720.

SPECIAL TOPICS

1509 [DELMOTTE, W. A.] *Drawings to Milton's* Paradise Lost. London, 1856. [474 plates.]

1510 [DORÉ, Gustave] Vaughan, R., ed. *Milton's Paradise Lost. Illustrated by Gustave Doré.* London: Cassell [1866].

1511 [FLATTERS, J. J.] *The Paradise Lost of Milton. Translated into Fifty-four Designs by J. J. Flatters.* London, 1843.

1511A FRANSON, J. Karl. "Christ on the Pinnacle: Interpretative Illustrations of the Crisis in *Paradise Regained.*" *Milton Q,* 10 (1976), 48–53.

1511B FRYE, Roland M. "Milton's Paradise Lost and the Visual Arts." *PAPS,* 120 (1976), 233–244.

1512 [FUSELI, H.] See **1498.**

1513 GARBER, Marjorie. "Fallen Landscape: The Art of Milton and Poussin." *ELR,* 5 (1975), 96–124.

1514 GARDNER, Helen. "Milton's First Illustrator." *E & S,* 9 (1956), 27–38. [I.e., de Medina. Reprinted in 831.]

1515 [HAMILTON, W.] See **1498.**

1516 [HAYMAN, Francis] Newton's edition of *Paradise Lost,* 1749 **(327).**

1517 HUGHES, Merritt Y. "Some Illustrators of Milton: The Expulsion from Paradise." *JEGP,* 60 (1961), 670–679. [Reprinted in **476.**]

1518 HUNT, John Dixon. "Milton's Illustrators." *John Milton: Introductions.* Ed. John Broadbent. Cambridge: Cambridge Univ. Press, 1973. pp. 208–224.

1519 [JOUBERT, F.] *Paradise Lost by John Milton. Illustrated by Thirty-eight Designs in Outline. Thirty-Four of the Plates Engraved by the Artist and Four by F. Joubert.* London: Hardwicke & Bogue, 1879.

1519A KOEHLER, G. Stanley. "Milton and the Art of Landscape." *Milton Studies VIII* (1975), 3–40.

1519B LABRIOLA, Albert C. "The Aesthetics of Self-Diminution: Christian Iconography and *Paradise Lost.*" *Milton Studies VII* (1975), 267–311.

1520 [MARTIN, John] *The Paradise Lost of John Milton, with Illustrations Designed and Engraved by John Martin.* 2 vols. London: S. Prowett, 1827.

1521 [MEDINA, John Baptist de] *Paradise Lost,* 4th ed., 1688 **(328).**

1521A MILLER, Leo. *Milton's Portraits.* A special issue of the *Milton Quarterly.* Athens, Ohio: Ohio Univ. Press, 1976.

1522 POINTON, Marcia R. *Milton and English Art.* Toronto: Univ. of Toronto Press, 1970.

1523 SHAWCROSS, John T. "The First Illustrations for *Paradise Lost.*" *Milton Q,* 9 (1975), 43–46.

1524 SPENCER, Jeffrey B. "Milton's Epic Landscapes: Responses to the Classical Baroque." *Heroic Nature: Ideal Landscapes in English Poetry from Marvell to Thomson.* Evanston: Northwestern Univ. Press, 1973, pp. 101–136.

1525 SVENDSEN, Kester. "John Martin and the Expulsion Scene of *Paradise Lost.*" *SEL,* 1 (1961), 63–73.

1526 [THORNHILL, Sir James] See **1508.**

1527 TRAPP, J. B. "Iconography." *John Milton: Introductions.* Ed. John Broadbent. Cambridge: Cambridge Univ. Press, 1973, pp. 162–185.

1528 TRAPP, J. B. "The Iconology of the Fall of Man." *Approaches to Paradise Lost: The York Tercentenary Lectures.* Ed. C. A. Patrides **(491)**, pp. 223–265.

1529 [TURNER, J. M. W.] Brydges' edition of *Poetical Works,* 1835 **(274)**.

1530 [WESTALL, R.] *The Poetical Works of John Milton,* 1794–1797 **(289)**.

1531 WITTREICH, Joseph A., Jr. "A Catalogue of Blake's Illustrations to Milton." *Calm of Mind.* Ed. J. A. Wittreich **(500)**, pp. 331–342.

1532 WITTREICH, Joseph A., Jr. " 'Divine Countenance': Blake's Portrait and Portrayals of Milton." *HLQ,* 38 (1975), 125–160.

1533 WITTREICH, Joseph A., Jr. "Illustrators of *Paradise Regained* and Their Subjects (1713–1816)." *Calm of Mind.* Ed. J. A. Wittreich **(500)**, pp. 309–329.

1534 WITTREICH, Joseph A., Jr. "Milton's First Illustrator." *SCN,* 32 (1974), 70–71.

1535 WITTREICH, Joseph A., Jr. "William Blake: Illustrator-Interpreter of *Paradise Regained.*" *Calm of Mind.* Ed. J. A. Wittreich **(500)**, pp. 93–132.

Fame and Influence

1536 ADAMS, Robert M. *Ikon: John Milton and the Modern Critics.* Ithaca: Cornell University Press, 1955. [Cornell, 1966]†

1537 ALPERS, Paul J. "The Milton Controversy." *Twentieth-Century Literature in Retrospect.* Ed. Reuben A. Brower. Cambridge: Harvard Univ. Press, 1971, pp. 269–298.

1538 ARNOLD, Matthew. "A French Critic on Milton." *Mixed Essays.* London: Smith, Elder, 1879.

1539 BARKER, Arthur E. " '... And on His Crest Sat Horror': Eighteenth Century Interpretations of Milton's Sublimity and His Satan." *UTQ,* 11 (1942), 421–436.

1540 BARKER, Arthur E. "Seven Types of Milton Criticism." *UTQ,* 25 (1956), 494–506.

1541 BERGONZI, Bernard. "Criticism and the Milton Controversy." *The Living Milton: Essays by Various Hands.* Ed. Frank Kermode **(486)**, pp. 162–180.

1541A BEYETTE, Kent. "Milton and Pope's *The Rape of the Lock.*" *SEL,* 16 (1976), 421–436.

1542 BLONDEL, Jacques. "Sur dix années de critique miltonienne." *EA,* 16 (1963), 38–53.

1543 BOLLIER, E. P. "T. S. Eliot and John Milton: A Problem in Criticism." *TSE,* 8 (1958), 165–192.

1544 BRINKLEY, Florence. "Milton in French Literature of the Nineteenth Century." *UTQ,* 27 (1958), 243–255.

1545 BRISMAN, Leslie. *Milton's Poetry of Choice and Its Romantic Heirs.* Ithaca and London: Cornell Univ. Press, 1973.

1546 BROADBENT, J. B. "Milton and Arnold." *Essays in Criticism,* 6 (1956), 404–417.

1547 BROOKS, Cleanth. "Milton and Critical Re-Estimates." *PMLA,* 66 (1951), 1045–1054. [Written as opposing view to **1609**.]

1548 BROOKS, Cleanth. "Milton and the New Criticism." *SR,* 59 (1951), 1–22. [Reprinted in *A Shaping Joy.* New York: Harcourt, Brace, Jovanovich, 1971.]

1549 COBB, Carl W. "Milton and Blank Verse in Spain." *PQ,* 42 (1963), 264–267.

1550 COLLINS, John Churton. "Miltonic Myths and Their Authors." *Studies in Poetry and Criticism.* London: Bell, 1905, pp. 167–203.

1551 [COLMAN, *George*]. *Comus: A Masque. Altered from Milton.* London: T. Lowndes et al., 1772.

1552 COOPER, Lane. "The Abyssinian Paradise in Coleridge and Milton." *MP,* 3 (1906), 327–332.

1553 CURRAN, Stuart. "The Mental Pinnacle: *Paradise Regained* and the Romantic Four-Book Epic." *Calm of Mind.* Ed. J. A. Wittreich (**500**), pp. 133–162.

1553A CURRAN, Stuart. *Shelley's Annus Mirabilis: The Maturing of an Epic Vision.* San Marino, California: Huntington Library Publications, 1975.

1554 [DALTON, *John*]. *Comus, a Mask: (Now Adapted to the Stage) As Altered from Milton's Mask at Ludlow Castle.* London: R. Dodsley, 1738.

1555 DRYDEN, John. *The State of Innocence, and Fall of Man: An Opera Written in Heroic Verse.* London: Herringman, 1677.

1556 ELIOT, T. S. *Milton.* Oxford: Oxford Univ. Press, 1947. [Reprinted in *SR,* 56 (1948), 185–209, in *T. S. Eliot: Selected Prose.* Ed. John Hayward (Penguin, 1953), in *On Poetry and Poets* (Faber, 1957), and in **499**. This essay and "A Note on the Verse of John Milton" (**1254**) were reprinted by Faber under the title *Milton: Two Studies.* [Noonday]†]

1557 EMPSON, William. "Milton and Bentley." *Some Versions of Pastoral.* London: Chatto & Windus, 1935, pp. 149–194. [Penguin, 1966]† [Reprinted in **489**.]

1558 FOGLE, French. "Milton Lost and Regained." *HLQ,* 15 (1952), 351–369.

1559 FOGLE, Richard Harter. "Johnson and Coleridge on Milton." *Bucknell Review,* 14 (1966), i, 26–32. [The emphasis is on Coleridge's response to Johnson *and* Milton.]

1560 FRENCH, J. Milton. "Moseley's Advertisements of Milton's Poems, 1650–1660." *HLQ,* 25 (1962), 337–345.

1561 GILBERT, Allan H. "Critics of Mr. C. S. Lewis on Milton's Satan." *SAQ,* 47 (1948), 216–225.

1562 GILBERT, Allan H. "Some Critical Opinions on Milton." *SP,* 33 (1936), 523–533.

1563 GOOD, John Walter. *Studies in the Milton Tradition.* Urbana: Univ. of Illinois Press, 1915.

1564 GORDON, R. K. "Keats and Milton." *MLR,* 42 (1947), 434–446.

1565 HAVENS, Raymond D. *The Influence of Milton on English Poetry.* Cambridge: Harvard Univ. Press, 1922.

1566 HERTZ, Neil H. "Wordsworth and the Tears of Adam." *Studies in Romanticism,* 7 (1967), 15–33.

SPECIAL TOPICS

1567 HONAN, Park. "Belial upon Setebos." *TSL,* 9 (1964), 87–98. [Browning's meaning in "Caliban upon Setebos" cannot be seen "until we know the Miltonic part of it." The soliloquy draws heavily on Belial's address, *PL,* II, 119–225.]

1568 HOWARD, Leon. "Early American Copies of Milton." *Huntington Library Bulletin,* 7 (1935), 169–179.

1569 HOWELL, A. C. "Milton's Mortal Remains and Their Literary Echoes." *BSTCF,* 4 (1963), ii, 17–30.

1570 JENNY, Gustav. *Miltons* Verlorenes Paradies *in der deutschen Literatur des 18. Jahrhunderts.* St. Gallen: Zollikofer, 1890.

1571 JONES, Frederick L. "Shelley and Milton." *SP,* 49 (1952), 488–519.

1572 LANDOR, Walter Savage. *Imaginary Conversations of Literary Men and Statesmen.* 5 vols. London: Taylor & Hessey, 1824–1829. ["Milton and Andrew Marvell." "Southey and Landor." "Andrew Marvell and Bishop Parker." "Galileo, Milton, and a Dominican."]

1573 MCALISTER, Floyd L. "Milton and the Anti-Academics." *JEGP,* 61 (1962), 779–787.

1574 MCLAUGHLIN, Elizabeth T., with the assistance of D. H. Raffensperger. "Coleridge and Milton." *SP,* 61 (1964), 545–572. [In contrast to modern critics whose theories derive from Coleridge, Coleridge himself saw Milton as a great exemplar of organic unity, etc.]

1575 MARTIN, Leonard Cyril. "Thomas Warton and the Early Poems of Milton." *Proceedings of the Bibliographical Association,* 20 (1934), 24–43.

1576 MURRAY, Patrick. *Milton: The Modern Phase: A Study of Twentieth-Century Criticism.* London: Longmans, 1967.

1577 MYERS, Robert Manson. *Handel, Dryden, and Milton: Being a Series of Observations on the Poems of Dryden and Milton, as Alter'd and Adapted by Various Hands, and Set to Musick by Mr. Handel, to Which Are Added Authentick Texts of Several of Mr. Handel's Oratorios.* Cambridge: Bowes & Bowes, 1956.

1578 NELSON, James G. *The Sublime Puritan: Milton and the Victorians.* Madison: Univ. of Wisconsin Press, 1963. [Detailed study of Milton's fame and influence to the later nineteenth century, "when Victorian criticism of the poet begins to merge with our own."]

1579 ORAS, Ants. *Milton's Editors and Commentators from Patrick Hume to Henry John Todd (1695–1801). A Study in Critical Views and Methods.* London: Oxford Univ. Press; Tartu: Univ. of Tartu (Dorpat), 1931. Rev. ed., New York: Haskell House, 1967. [Adds a postscript on Bentley's Milton. Reprinted by Oxford Univ. Press, 1970.]

1580 ORAS, Ants. "The Multitudinous Orb: Some Miltonic Elements in Shelley." *MLQ,* 16 (1955), 247–257.

1581 PARKER, William R. *Milton's Contemporary Reputation, an Essay, together with a Tentative List of Printed Allusions to Milton, 1641–1674, and Facsimile Reproductions of Five Contemporary Pamphlets Written in Answer to Milton.* Columbus: Ohio State Univ. Press, 1940.

1582 PEERS, E. Allison. "Milton in Spain." *SP,* 23 (1926), 169–183.

1583 PELLETIER, Robert R. "Shelley's Ahasuerus and Milton's Satan." *N&Q,* 7 (1960), 259–260.

SPECIAL TOPICS

1584 POMMER, Henry F. *Milton and Melville.* Pittsburgh: Univ. of Pittsburgh Press, 1950.

1585 RABEN, Joseph. "Milton's Influence on Shelley's Translation of Dante's 'Matilda Gathering Flowers'." *RES,* 14 (1963), 142–156.

1586 SANKEY, Benjamin T. "Coleridge on Milton's Satan." *PQ,* 43 (1964), 504–508. [Coleridge's sound approach to Satan derived from (1) his effort to distinguish the noumenal from the phenomenal world, and (2) the political problem of Napoleon (strength from selfish principles).]

1587 SAURAT, Denis. *Blake and Milton.* Bordeaux: Cadoret, 1920, [Reprinted, London: Stanley Nott, 1935.]

1588 SCHERPBIER, H. *Milton in Holland: A Study in the Literary Relations of England and Holland before 1730.* Amsterdam: H. J. Paris, 1933.

1589 SCHULZ, Max F. "Coleridge, Milton, and Lost Paradise." *N&Q,* N.S. 6 (1959), 143–144.

1590 SENSABAUGH, George F. *Milton in Early America.* Princeton: Princeton Univ. Press, 1964.

1591 SENSABAUGH, George F. *That Grand Whig, Milton.* Stanford: Stanford Univ. Press, 1952.

1592 SHERBURN, George W. "The Early Popularity of Milton's *Minor Poems.* " *MP,* 17 (1919–1920), 259–278, 515–540.

1593 SLOANE, William. "Chaucer, Milton, and the Rev. William Stukeley, M.D." *N&Q,* N.S., 7 (1960), 220–222.

1594 SMITH, Logan Pearsall. *Milton and His Modern Critics.* London: Oxford Univ. Press, 1940. [Reprinted, Boston: Little, Brown, 1941.]

1595 STANTON, Robert. *"Typee* and Milton: Paradise Well Lost." *MLN,* 74 (1959), 407–411.

1596 STEVENS, Albert K. "Milton and Chartism." *PQ,* 12 (1933), 377–388.

1597 TAYLER, Irene. "Say First! What Mov'd Blake? Blake's *Comus* Designs and *Milton.* " *Blake's Sublime Allegory.* Ed. Stuart Curran and Joseph A. Wittreich, Jr. Madison and London: Univ. of Wisconsin Press, 1973, pp. 233–258.

1598 TELLEEN, John Martin. *Milton dans la littérature française.* Paris: Hachette, 1904.

1599 THALER, Alwin. "Milton in the Theatre." *SP,* 17 (1920), 269–308. [Reprinted in *Shakspere's Silences.* Cambridge: Harvard Univ. Press, 1929, pp. 209–256.] [Stagings of *Comus.*]

1600 TILLYARD, E. M. W. "Arnold on Milton." *Studies in Milton* (569), pp. 1–7.

1601 WATSON, Tommy G. "Johnson and Hazlitt on the Imagination in Milton." *SoQ,* 2 (1964), 123–133. [Compares Johnson's *Life of Milton* and Hazlitt's *Lecture on Shakespeare and Milton.*]

1602 WHITE, T. Holt, ed. *Areopagitica. . . . To Which Is Subjoined a Tract Sur la Liberté de la presse, imité de l'Anglois de Milton par le Comte de Mirabeau.* London: R. Hunter, 1819.

1603 WILKIE, Brian. *Romantic Poets and Epic Tradition.* Madison and Milwaukee: Univ. of Wisconsin Press, 1965. [The epic is approached not as a genre but as a tradition, and *Paradise Lost* is discussed often as a key word in that tradition.]

1604 WITTREICH, Joseph A., Jr. *Angel of Apocalypse: Blake's Idea of Milton.* Madison: Univ. of Wisconsin Press, 1974.

1605 WITTREICH, Joseph A., Jr. " 'Divine Countenance': Blake's Portrait and Portrayals of Milton." *HLQ,* 38 (1975), 125–160. [Blake's conception of Milton as revealed in his iconic and verbal depictions of Milton.]

1606 WITTREICH, Joseph A., Jr. "Opening the Seals: Blake's Epics and the Milton Tradition." *Blake's Sublime Allegory.* Ed. Stuart Curran and Joseph A. Wittreich, Jr. Madison and London: Univ. of Wisconsin Press, 1973, pp. 23–58.

1607 WITTREICH, Joseph A., Jr., ed. *The Romantics on Milton: Formal Essays and Critical Asides.* Cleveland and London: The Press of Case Western Reserve Univ., 1970.

1608 WOLFE, Don M. "Milton and Mirabeau." *PMLA,* 49 (1934), 1116–1128.

1609 WOODHOUSE, A. S. P. "The Historical Criticism of Milton." *PMLA,* 66 (1951), 1033–1044. [Written in opposition to **1547.**]

Miscellaneous

1610 ARTHOS, John. *Milton and the Italian Cities.* New York: Barnes & Noble, 1968. [Discusses the social and intellectual life of the cities which Milton visited during his Italian journey. Part I: Florence, Rome, Naples, Venice. Part II: Milton and Monteverdi.]

1611 BAUMGARTNER, Paul R. "Milton and Patience." *SP,* 60 (1963), 203–213.

1612 BUSH, Douglas. "Calculus Racked Him." *SEL,* 6 (1966), 1–6. [An objection to Røstvig's numerological interpretation of *Comus* and the Nativity Ode in *The Hidden Sense* (**1639**). Cf. Røstvig's reply and Bush's rejoinder, *SEL,* 7 (1967), 191–194.]

1613 DUNCAN, Joseph E. *Milton's Earthly Paradise: A Historical Study of Eden.* Minneapolis: Univ. of Minnesota Press, 1972.

1614 EISENSTEIN, Sergei. *Film Form and The Film Sense.* Trans. Jay Leyda. New York: Meridian Books, 1957.† [Pp. 58–62 of *The Film Sense.*] [*PL* as a resource for studying montage and audio-visual relationships.]

1614A FISH, Stanley E. "Interpreting the *Variorum. Critical Inquiry,* 2 (1975–1976), 465–485. [See the responses by Douglas Bush and Steven Mailloux and the author's reply in *Critical Inquiry* 3 (1976–1977), 179–196.]

1615 FOGLE, French R. "Milton as Historian." *Milton and Clarendon: Two Papers on 17th Century English Historiography Presented at a Seminar Held at The Clark Library on December 12, 1964.* Los Angeles: Clark Memorial Library, 1965, pp. 1–20.

1616 FRENCH, J. Milton. "Milton as Satirist." *PMLA,* 51 (1936), 414–429.

1617 FRYE, Northrop. "The Revelation to Eve." *Paradise Lost: A Tercentenary Tribute.* Ed. Balachandra Rajan (**494**), pp. 18–47. [Male and female motifs as mythopoeic polarities in Milton's poetry. Not limited to *Paradise Lost.*]

1618 GILBERT, Allan H. "Milton on the Position of Women." *MLR,* 15 (1920), 240–264.

SPECIAL TOPICS

1619 GROSE, Christopher. "Milton on Ramist Similitude." *Seventeenth-Century Imagery.* Ed. Earl Miner. Berkeley, Los Angeles, London: Univ. of California Press, 1971, pp. 103–116.

1620 HANFORD, James Holly. "Milton and the Art of War." *SP,* 18 (1921), 232–266. [Reprinted in **526.**]

1621 HANFORD, James Holly. "The Temptation Motive in Milton." *SP,* 15 (1918), 176–194. [Reprinted in **526.**]

1622 HUGHES, Merritt Y. "Lydian Airs." *MLN,* 40 (1925), 129–137. [Milton's attitude toward the Platonic doctrine of music's effect on character. Reprinted in **529.**]

1623 HUGHES, Merritt Y. "Milton's Eikon Basilike." *Calm of Mind.* Ed. Joseph A. Wittreich, Jr. **(500),** pp. 1–24. ["Images" of Kingship in Milton's poetry.]

1623A KER, W. P. ["Simple, Sensuous, and Passionate."] *Form and Style in Poetry.* London: Macmillan, 1928, pp. 175–184.

1624 KRANIDAS, Thomas. *The Fierce Equation: A Study of Milton's Decorum.* The Hague: Mouton, 1965. [A study of the prose and *PL* through the concept of decorum, broadly defined.]

1624A LANDY, Marcia. "A Free and Open Encounter: Milton and the Modern Reader." *Milton Studies IX* (1976), 3–36. [Particularly concerned with Milton's presentation of women. cf. **1628.**]

1625 LANDY, Marcia. "Kinship and the Role of Women in *Paradise Lost.*" *Milton Studies IV* (1972), 3–18. [Cf. **1628.**]

1626 LE COMTE, Edward. "Milton as Satirist and Wit." *Th' Upright Heart and Pure.* Ed. Amadeus P. Fiore **(483),** pp. 45–59. [Reprinted in **538.**]

1627 LEWALSKI, Barbara Kiefer. "Milton on Learning and the Learned-Ministry Controversy." *HLQ,* 24 (1961), 267–281.

1628 LEWALSKI, Barbara K. "Milton on Women—Yet Once More." *Milton Studies VI* (1975), 3–20.

1629 LEWALSKI, Barbara K. "Milton: Revaluations of Romance." *Four Essays on Romance.* Ed. Herschel Baker. Cambridge: Harvard Univ. Press, 1971. pp. 55–70.

1630 LONG, Ann B. " 'She May Have More Shapes Than One': Milton and the Modern Idea That Truth Changes." *Milton Studies VI* (1975), 85–99. [Milton's idea of the progressive revelation of truth is compared to modern scientific theories of the relativity of truth. Especially pertinent to Raphael's comments on knowledge within bounds in *PL* VIII.]

1631 MAYNARD, Winifred. "Milton and Music." *John Milton: Introductions.* Ed. John Broadbent. Cambridge: Cambridge Univ. Press, 1973, pp. 226–252.

1632 MOHL, Ruth. "Milton and the Idea of Perfection." *Studies in Spenser, Milton, and the Theory of Monarchy* New York: Columbia Univ. Press, 1949, pp. 94–132.

1633 MOLLENKOTT, Virginia R. "Milton's Technique of Multiple Choice." *Milton Studies VI* (1975), 101–111. [The unresolved choice of alternative possibilities in the major poems.]

1634 MORKAN, Joel. "Wrath and Laughter: Milton's Ideas on Satire." *SP,* 69 (1972), 475–495.

1635 MORRIS, John N. "Milton and the Imagination of Time." *SAQ,* 67 (1968), 649–658.

1636 OGDEN, H. V. S. "The Principles of Variety and Contrast in Seventeenth-Century Aesthetics, and Milton's Poetry." *JHI*, 10 (1949), 159–182.

1637 RAJAN, Balachandra. "Simple, Sensuous, and Passionate." *RES*, 21 (1945), 289–301. [Reprinted in **476.** The implications of Milton's description of poetry as "simple, sensuous, and passionate."]

1638 ROSCELLI, William J. "The Metaphysical Milton (1625–1631)." *TSLL*, 8 (1967), 463–484.

1639 RØSTVIG, Maren-Sofie. "The Hidden Sense: Milton and the Neoplatonic Method of Numerical Composition." *The Hidden Sense and Other Essays.* Oslo: Universitetsforlaget; New York: Humanities Press, 1963, pp. 1–112. [Ch. 3 deals specifically with Milton, primarily with the Nativity Ode and *Comus.*]

1640 RØSTVIG, Maren-Sofie. "Renaissance Numerology: Acrostics or Criticism?" *EIC*, 16 (1966), 6–21. [Discusses Milton at some length.]

1641 SAMUEL, Irene. "Milton on Comedy and Satire." *HLQ*, 35 (1972), 107–130.

1642 SAMUEL, Irene. "Milton on Learning and Wisdom." *PMLA*, 64 (1949), 708–723.

1643 SCHULTZ, Howard. *Milton and Forbidden Knowledge.* New York: Modern Language Association of America, 1955.

1644 SENSABAUGH, George F. "Milton on Learning." *SP*, 43 (1946), 258–272.

1645 SIEGEL, Paul N. "Milton and the Humanist Attitude toward Women." *JHI*, 11 (1950), 42–53.

1646 SIRLUCK, Ernest. "Some Recent Changes in the Chronology of Milton's Poems." *JEGP*, 60 (1961), 773–785. [*SA*, Sonnet 7, and *Ad Patrem.* Reprinted in **490,** pp. 165–177.]

1647 STARNES, D. T. "Proper Names in Milton: New Annotations." *A Tribute to G. C. Taylor.* Ed. Arnold Williams. Chapel Hill: Univ. of North Carolina Press, 1952. pp. 38–61.

1648 WOLFE, Don M. "Limits of Miltonic Toleration." *JEGP*, 60 (1961), 834–846. [Milton's attitude toward Catholicism and Judaism.]

1649 WOLFE, Don M. "Milton's Conception of the Ruler." *SP*, 33 (1936), 253–272. [Discussions of Charles I, Cromwell, and the ruler in *PL.*]

1650 WOLFE, Don M. "Milton, Lilburne, and the People." *MP*, 31 (1934), 253–272.

INDEX

INDEX

INDEX

INDEX

INDEX

INDEX

INDEX

INDEX

INDEX

NOTES